HOMEMADE
ICE CREAM
naturally

Publisher: George Barber

© Mark Young and Lesley Howard Murdoch
Published by Bay Books
61–69 Anzac Parade
Kensington NSW 2033
Card number and ISBN 1 86256 075 7

BB87

Food styling: Christa Osbeck
Food preparation: Mark Young and Christa Osbeck

HOMEMADE
ICE CREAM
naturally

MARK YOUNG & LESLEY HOWARD MURDOCH

Photography Leonard Ozbeck

BAY BOOKS
SYDNEY & LONDON

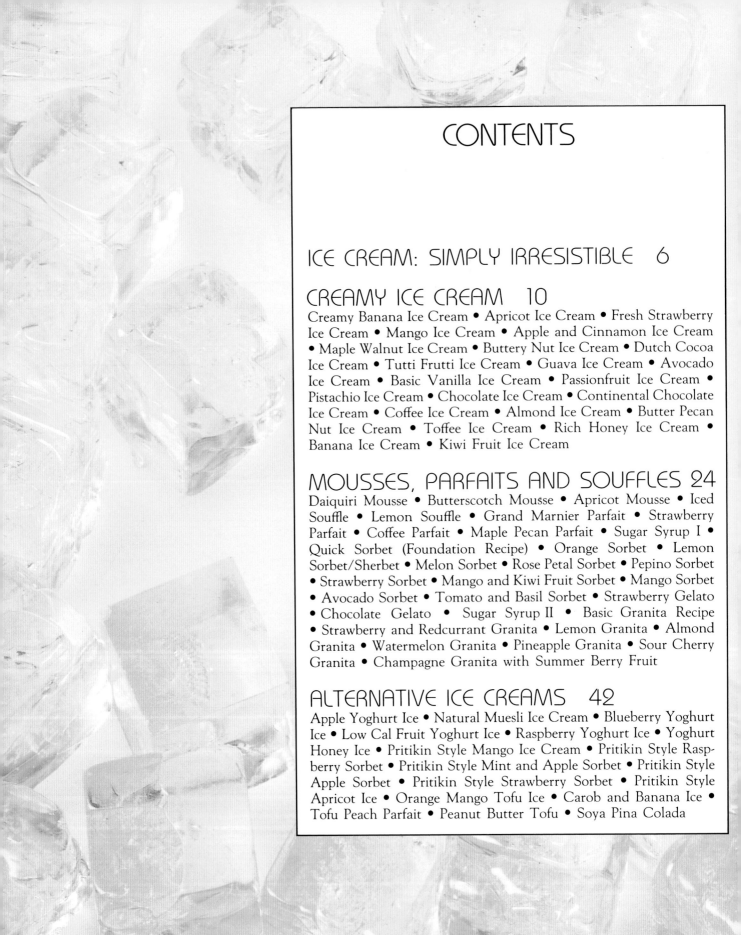

CONTENTS

◇ ICE CREAM: SIMPLY ◇ IRRESISTIBLE

Few things in life taste better than a scoop of homemade ice cream or a fresh fruity sorbet. Why not indulge yourself, your family and friends with delicious iced desserts using natural, nutritious ingredients, an ice cream maker and a little time?

Homemade Ice Cream, Naturally is filled with irresistible recipes for ice creams, gelati, sorbets, sherbets, mousses, parfaits and iced drinks.

Most recipes can be simply and easily prepared at home with a time-saving ice cream maker, whilst others only need to be still-frozen just the way our grandmas made their iced delights.

WHAT'S SO GOOD ABOUT HOMEMADE ICE CREAM?

You can taste the freshness in every scoop of homemade ice cream. It is all natural. You don't need any additives to extend shelf life: your confections are unlikely to have a shelf life! If homemade ice cream lasts a day, you'll be lucky.

Tasting good isn't enough in these health-conscious, diet-fad days. What you eat has to be good for you, too. Ice cream and iced desserts prepared with fresh milk, cream, eggs and fruit plus nuts and honey are very nutritious. Bursting with natural ingredients, these foods can play a useful part in a healthy diet.

BACK TO BASICS: WHAT IS IN THESE ICED DESSERTS?

The ingredients are all natural — cream or milk, eggs and sugar in ice cream: fruits and egg whites in sorbets and sherbets.

CREAM   Rich ice cream is usually cream based. There are several different types of cream available labelled according to the amount of butterfat that they contain.

Type	Per cent butterfat (minimum)
AUSTRALIA	
Reduced cream	25%
Cream	35%
Thickened cream	35%
Whipping cream	40% (Qld.)
	42% (W.A.)
Rich cream	48% (Vic., W.A., S.A., Tas.)
UK	
Single cream	18%
Whipping cream	35%
Double cream	48%

Most of the recipes in this book that require cream, use cream containing 35 per cent butterfat. In those recipes calling for milk, you can make a creamier version by substituting cream for some of the milk content. To make a drier, firmer ice cream, slightly reduce the amount of cream and egg yolks.

MILK   Recipes using milk make a harder and more crystalline dessert than those with cream. The type of milk you choose affects the flavour. The recipes in this book were prepared using homogenised pasteurised milk. If you substitute skimmed milk, your ice cream will be icier. Buttermilk also has less fat but is thick and has a refreshing acidity that blends well with many fruit ices.

For vegetarians, soya bean milk is ideal. It is low in kilojoules and cholesterol-free. Yoghurt makes a slightly piquant flavoured ice on its own or blended with milk, creams or even soft cheeses.

Tofu is another substitute popular with vegetarians and people cutting down on cholesterol and kilojoules. It is low in fat and high in protein. Some varieties have a coarse texture. Choose a creamy smooth brand like Silken Tofu for making ice creams.

From top clockwise: Apple Yoghurt Ice; Low Cal Fruit Yoghurt Ice and Natural Muesli Ice Cream

SUGAR   If you freeze a litre of cream it will be rock hard and impossible to serve. Sugar in some form is essential. It not only sweetens the flavour but controls the softness of your ice cream. Too much and your ice cream won't freeze; too little and you may need a pick axe. Undissolved sugar will give the ice cream a grainy texture.

Granulated sugar and caster sugar are used in most recipes. Some, however, call for brown sugar. Liquid sweeteners such as honey or maple syrup give ice creams a flavour all their own. In some recipes, the kilojoule conscious can substitute artificial sweeteners. As a rough guide, three or four sweeteners equal about 25 grams of sugar. It's worth remembering that artificial sweeteners lose some of their sweetness when heated, so it's a good idea to add them after any cooking. The sweetener used in the Pritikin recipes in this book is apple juice concentrate.

CAN YOU EAT ICE CREAM AND WATCH YOUR WEIGHT?

Yes. Ice creams and diets aren't mutually exclusive. They can be eaten in moderation by people trying to lose weight. One scoop of vanilla ice cream (custard-style) contains about 574 kJ whereas a standard, fruity-flavoured carton of yoghurt contains about 838 kJ.

There are also a number of alternative ways of making ice creams that greatly reduce the fat and sugar content — welcome news for followers of Pritikin style diets, diabetics and heart patients. Just take a look at our alternative ice cream chapter for all your options.

Lemon Sorbet and Orange Sorbet

WHY MAKE ICE CREAM?

The answer is simple: it's fun and it's easy these days especially with the latest ice cream makers available. An ice cream maker continually churns as it freezes, aerating the mixture and preventing ice crystals from forming.

If you haven't already succumbed and bought a machine, now is the time to weigh up the pros and cons. They do produce the smoothest ice cream in the shortest time but to make the most of your investment, it's important to use it fairly often.

Several types are available, from the top-of-the-range domestic models with a built-in freezing unit, fixed bowl and removable bowls for extra batches; to the popularly priced models, either those with a removable dish you freeze before churning or the small electric models with a rechargeable battery that churn the ice cream inside your own freezer.

Before buying, check the features of each type. Look at the noise level, the amount of ice cream you could make in a day, the preparation time (recharging the battery or freezing the dish) and ease of cleaning. One feature to look for, particularly, is a paddle that lifts clear of the ice cream before it freezes hard.

WHAT DO YOU NEED IN THE WAY OF KITCHEN EQUIPMENT?

☐ Metric measuring jug, cups and spoons
☐ Scales are a must. Always weigh or measure out the ingredients, especially sugar
☐ A double boiler (for custard making)
☐ Utensils such as wooden spoons, spatula and nylon sieve
☐ A sugar thermometer will save hovering and worrying about the right temperature
☐ An electric blender
☐ Metal or plastic containers with lids for freezing and storing the ice creams
☐ A decorative serving container for those iced desserts like mousses, parfaits and souffles, which go straight from freezer to table.

Four popular ice cream makers from Kenwood, Breville, Philips and Black & Decker. The Kenwood unit has a compressor and is like a small freezer; the Breville has a rechargeable battery and fits inside your freezer; both Philips and Black & Decker have disks that you freeze and then place in the ice cream maker.

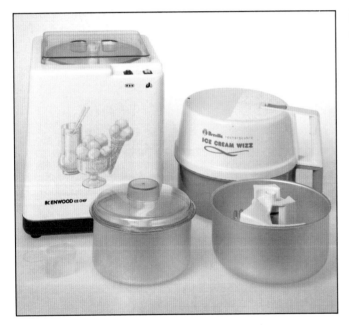

HOW LONG TO FREEZE?

There's no easy answer to this question. The time depends on the type of ice cream maker, the temperature of your equipment, whether you chilled the ingredients, the weather, the temperature in your kitchen, the quantity of ice cream and even the shape of your container . . . Manufacturers give approximate times in their ice cream maker manuals. For still-freezing, allow two to three hours. To avoid the disappointment of half frozen ices, make them the day before you need them, allowing time for the flavours to ripen and the texture to form properly.

HOW GOOD IS STILL-FREEZING?

You don't need modern labour saving devices. Still-freezing makes absolutely delicious ice cream if you beat it right. Continual and regular stirring is needed to prevent the formation of ice crystals and speed freezing. Simply stir two or three times during freezing time by beating the edges of the mixture into the centre with a fork or rotary hand beater.

FREEZING TIPS

- ☐ Chill your equipment — bowls, whisks, spatulas — before use.
- ☐ Cool your custard-base mixture quickly by plunging the bowl into a basin of cold water or ice cubes.
- ☐ Chill all other mixture in the refrigerator before placing in ice cream maker.
- ☐ Turn the setting of your freezer to its coldest or quick freeze position.
- ☐ Metal containers will freeze ice creams etc. faster than plastic. But don't use metal with acid fruits as the acid will react.
- ☐ Ice cream will still-freeze faster in a shallow, metal container.
- ☐ If using the freezer, place one side of the container in touch with the freezer sides or base. Leave space for the air to circulate around the container.
- ☐ Homemade ice cream should be made and frozen at least a day before eating to allow the ice cream to set and ripen.
- ☐ Ice cream should always be removed from the freezer and kept in the fridge for 30 minutes to allow *slow* softening before serving.

Still freezing ice cream

1   Tip into a chilled container

2   Well-timed beating aerates the ice cream better than using a food processor

3   Return the mixture to freezer to firm again

4   Place in a serving dish

American style ice cream

1   *Blend ingredients for 30 seconds on high*

2   *Pour mixture into ice cream maker and freeze following the manufacturer's instructions*

AMERICAN-STYLE ICE CREAMS

These creamy ice creams are the ideal summer dessert that's popular all year round. Based on cream, sugar and fresh fruit, they lend themselves to endless individual variations. Easy-to-make American-style ice creams need no cooking at all — just the freshest of ingredients create these creamy ice-creams.

CREAMY BANANA ICE CREAM

500 g barely ripe bananas	1 egg (65 g)
1½ tablespoons lemon juice	65 mL (¼ cup) milk
200 g caster sugar	465 mL cream

1   Quickly peel the bananas and blend at high speed for 30 seconds with the lemon juice and sugar.

2   Reduce speed before adding the egg, milk and 65 mL (¼ cup) cream. Blend a further 30 seconds.

3   Add the remaining 400 mL cream and blend for 20–30 seconds.

4   Pour the mixture into your ice cream maker and freeze quickly, following manufacturer's instructions.

5   Store frozen banana ice cream in an airtight container to retain its creamy white colour. Banana ice cream may brown slightly when exposed to air.

Makes 1 litre

APRICOT ICE CREAM

1 egg (65 g)	1 teaspoon vanilla essence
150 g caster sugar	175 g dried apricots, soaked
65 mL (¼ cup) milk	overnight and chilled
665 mL (2⅔ cups) cream	

1   Place the egg, sugar, milk, 65 mL (¼ cup) cream and vanilla in blender and process at low speed for about 30 seconds until smooth.

2   Drain the apricots, add to the blender and process a further 30 seconds.

3   Slowly add the remaining 600 mL cream and blend for 30 seconds.

4   Place the mixture in your ice cream maker and freeze, following the manufacturer's instructions.

Makes 1 litre

Fresh Strawberry Ice Cream; Creamy Banana Ice Cream and Apricot Ice Cream

FRESH STRAWBERRY ICE CREAM

300 g strawberries,
    washed and
    hulled
200 g caster sugar
1 egg (60 g)
65 mL (¼ cup) milk
465 mL cream
1 teaspoon vanilla essence

1   Blend the strawberries with the sugar until smooth.
2   Add the egg, milk, 65 mL (¼ cup) cream and vanilla to blender and process for 30 seconds.
3   Continue blending on low speed for 30 seconds while adding the remaining 400 mL cream.
4   Pour the mixture into your ice cream maker and freeze, following the manufacturer's instructions.
Makes 1 litre

MANGO ICE CREAM

Fresh is best for this recipe. However, mangoes aren't available all year round. Out of season substitute canned mangoes, drained and sieved. Do not use mango pulp as many brands contain too much sugar.

4 large, ripe mangoes or
    3 × 425 g cans mango
    segments
150 g caster sugar
1 egg (65 g)
465 mL cream
65 mL (¼ cup) milk
1 teaspoon vanilla essence

1   Peel, seed and sieve the mangoes to remove fibres (some varieties, such as Bowen, do not need sieving).
2   Place the mango puree and 75 g sugar in a double boiler and simmer gently for 15 minutes. Chill mango mixture in refrigerator for 30 minutes before using.
3   Place the egg, remaining sugar, 65 mL (¼ cup) cream, milk and vanilla essence in the blender and process for 30 seconds.
4   Add the chilled mango puree and blend for 15 seconds. Continue blending for about 30 seconds while adding the remaining 400 mL cream.
5   Place the mixture in your ice cream maker and freeze, following the manufacturer's instructions.
Makes 1 litre

APPLE AND CINNAMON ICE CREAM

3 large Granny Smith
    apples, unpeeled
65 mL (¼ cup) water
2 tablespoons cinnamon
180 g caster sugar
1 egg (65 g)
65 mL (¼ cup) milk
665 mL (2⅔ cups) cream
1 tablespoon vanilla essence

1   Core and dice the apples and place in a saucepan with the water, cinnamon and 70 g caster sugar.
2   Simmer over low heat for 15 minutes, then puree through a sieve and chill before using.
3   Place the egg, milk, 65 mL (¼ cup) cream, remaining 110 g sugar and the vanilla in a blender and process at low speed for about 30 seconds until the sugar is dissolved.
4   Slowly add the remaining 600 mL cream and blend a further 30 seconds.
5   Place the cream mixture in your ice cream maker, add the apple puree and freeze, following the manufacturer's instructions.
Makes 1 litre

MAPLE WALNUT ICE CREAM

Pure maple syrup is best for this recipe, but imitation maple syrup will make a delicious ice cream, too.

150 mL maple syrup
1 egg (60 g)
75 g caster sugar
125 mL (½ cup) milk
625 mL (2½ cups) cream
1 teaspoon vanilla essence
100 g chopped walnuts

1   Place the maple syrup, egg, sugar, milk, 125 mL (½ cup) cream and vanilla in blender and process on medium for about 30 seconds until the sugar is dissolved.
2   Continue blending while slowly adding the remaining 500 mL cream.
3   Place the mixture in your ice cream maker and freeze, following the manufacturer's instructions, for about 15 minutes.
4   When the mixture is half frozen, add the walnuts and freeze a further 25 minutes.
Makes 1 litre

Buttery Nut Ice Cream and Maple Walnut Ice Cream

BUTTERY NUT ICE CREAM

An ingenious way to encourage children — if they need any encouragement — to tuck into peanut butter.

200 g crunchy peanut butter
200 g caster sugar
250 mL (1 cup) milk
500 mL (2 cups) cream
1 egg (65 g)
1 tablespoon vanilla essence

1   Gently heat the peanut butter, sugar, 125 mL (½ cup) milk and 125 mL (½ cup) cream in a saucepan, stirring frequently until you have a smooth paste.

2   Chill mixture in refrigerator for 30 minutes before using.

3   Place the egg, remaining 125 mL (½ cup) milk, 125 mL (½ cup) cream and vanilla in blender and process for 20 seconds.

4   Slowly add the peanut paste and blend well.

5   Continue blending on slow speed for 75 seconds while adding the remaining cream.

6   Place the mixture in your ice cream maker and freeze, following the manufacturer's instructions. Check consistency at 25 minutes. Over-churning will make a buttery mixture rather than an ice cream.

Makes 1 litre

DUTCH COCOA ICE CREAM

2 eggs (65 g)
220 g caster sugar
65 mL (¼ cup) milk
665 mL (2⅔ cups) cream
1 teaspoon vanilla essence
3 tablespoons unsweetened
  cocoa powder

1　Place the eggs, sugar, milk, 65 mL (¼ cup) cream and vanilla in blender and process at medium speed for 30 seconds.
2　Slowly and carefully add the cocoa powder, continuing to blend for 30 seconds.
3　Add the remaining 600 mL cream and blend for 30 seconds.
4　Pour the mixture into your ice cream maker and freeze, following the manufacturer's instructions.
Makes 1 litre

TUTTI FRUTTI ICE CREAM

TUTTI FRUTTI
100 g sultanas, raisins and
  currants
30 g glace cherries, chopped
30 g crystallised pineapple,
  chopped
30 g crystallised orange and
  lemon, chopped
20 g angelica, chopped
3 tablespoons brandy

ICE CREAM
1 egg (60 g)
665 mL (2⅔ cups) cream
65 mL (¼ cup) milk
200 g caster sugar
1 teaspoon vanilla essence
1 teaspoon almond essence

1　Combine the fruit and brandy and soak, covered, for 4 hours or overnight.
2　Place the egg, 65 mL (¼ cup) cream, milk, sugar, vanilla and almond essences in blender and process on medium speed for about 30 seconds until the sugar has dissolved.
3　Continue blending on low speed for 30 seconds while adding the remaining 600 mL cream.
4　Pour the ice cream mixture into your ice cream maker, add the tutti frutti and freeze following the manufacturer's instructions.
Makes 1 litre

GUAVA ICE CREAM

There are several varieties of guava — some are pear shaped, others are more like an orange and one rather resembles a fig. The fruit is usually made into jam or canned because many people find its flavour rather insipid. Guavas, however, make wonderful ice creams and sorbets. The following recipe calls for fresh fruit peeled, seeded and pureed. If you substitute canned guavas, drain the syrup, wash and seed the fruit and use less sugar.

400 mL guava puree
165 g caster sugar
1 egg (65 g)
465 mL cream
65 mL (¼ cup) milk
½ teaspoon vanilla essence

1　Blend together the guava and sugar at high speed for 30 seconds.
2　Reduce speed to medium and add the egg, 65 mL (¼ cup) cream, milk and vanilla and blend a further 30 seconds.
3　Add the remaining 400 mL cream and blend for 20–30 seconds.
4　Place the mixture in your ice cream maker and freeze, following the manufacturer's instructions.
Makes 1 litre

AVOCADO ICE CREAM

2 large avocados, seeded and
  chopped
60 mL (¼ cup) orange juice
250 g caster sugar
2 teaspoons gelatine
500 mL (2 cups) cream

1　Combine avocado, orange juice and sugar in a blender and process at medium speed for 30 seconds.
2　Dissolve gelatine in 1 tablespoon warm water.
3　Pour gelatine and cream into a blender and blend for 30 seconds.
4　Place mixture in your ice cream maker and freeze, following the manufacturer's instructions.
Makes 1 litre

CUSTARD BASE ICE CREAMS

The following recipe for vanilla ice cream describes the basic procedure for egg custard bases, the foundation of many delightful ices. But first, some handy hints:

☐ To cook the custard accurately use a sugar thermometer and do not let the mixture exceed 85°C. Use a bain marie or double boiler to prevent overcooking.

☐ To test the custard without a thermometer stir with a wooden spoon and lift the spoon to a tilt so that the excess falls off. Use your finger to draw a line in the thin film left on the spoon. If the custard is cooked the line will hold its shape.

☐ If the custard is overcooked by heating too much, the eggs can curdle and the custard will look granular, like scrambled eggs. If this should happen, immediately remove the saucepan from the heat, take out the vanilla bean, add one tablespoon of cold milk and pour the custard into a blender or vitamiser. Process until smooth and then add the cream.

☐ To increase the flavour of all custard bases, after cooking the custard and having added the flavouring, let it mature overnight in the refrigerator before adding the cream and freezing.

Once you have mastered this basic recipe you can make many different flavours by simply adding one or two extra ingredients.

Custard base ice cream
1   Whisk a small amount of milk into egg and sugar mixture

2   Test custard for consistency — it should coat the back of spoon

BASIC VANILLA ICE CREAM

500 mL (2 cups) milk
1 vanilla bean split
   lengthways or 1½–2
   tablespoons vanilla
   essence
200 g caster sugar
6 egg yolks (50 g)
250 mL (1 cup) cream

1   Heat the milk in a saucepan with vanilla bean and 100 g sugar to boiling point, cover the pan, turn heat off and rest 15 minutes.
2   Beat the egg yolks and remaining 100 g sugar in a bowl until thick and light.
3   Bring the milk back to the boil and whisk a small amount into the egg and sugar mixture.
4   Remove the saucepan of milk from the heat and whisk the egg-sugar mix into it.
5   Return the saucepan to a low heat, stirring constantly; do not allow to boil. As the custard cooks it will thicken slowly. It should coat the back of a spoon when cooked.
6   Remove the pan from the heat and place in a bowl of cold water. Take out vanilla bean.
7   To prepare by hand, whip the cream until firm, then fold into the cooled custard, chill and freeze. If using an ice cream maker, pour the cream into the custard, chill and freeze, following the manufacturer's instructions.
Makes 1 litre

PASSIONFRUIT ICE CREAM

500 mL (2 cups) milk
6 egg yolks (60 g)
200 g sugar
200 mL cream
250 mL (1 cup) passionfruit
   pulp

1   Heat the milk.
2   Beat egg yolks with sugar.
3   Add egg/sugar mixture to the milk and cook until it thickens slightly.
4   Add the cream to the custard then chill.
5   Place mixture in your ice cream maker, process for 15 minutes, add passionfruit pulp and freeze, following the manufacturer's instructions.
Makes 1 litre

PISTACHIO ICE CREAM

The pale green pistachio has a delicate but discernible flavour. This ice cream is naturally pale greenish brown in colour, unlike the more attractive-looking commercial brands which probably contain green food colouring. A natural green colouring can, however, be obtained by squeezing the juice from freshly cooked spinach!

230 g shelled pistachios
25 g blanched almonds
200 g sugar
750 mL (3 cups) milk
6 egg yolks (50 g)

1   To prepare the pistachios, put the unsalted kernels in a bowl, pour in boiling water to cover and blanch for a few minutes. Drain and peel.
2   Place the pistachios and almonds in a food processor with 100 g sugar and blend for several seconds until a coarse grainy powder is formed.
3   Add nut powder to the milk in a saucepan over a high heat and bring to the boil, stirring all the time. Cover and remove from heat. Stand for 30 minutes.
4   Strain the milk into a fresh saucepan and bring to the boil.
5   Beat the egg yolks and remaining 100 g sugar to a ribbon consistency and whisk in some of the milk. Stir the egg-sugar mix back into the milk and cook on a low heat to thicken, for about 10 minutes; cool.
6   Place the mixture into your ice cream maker and freeze, following the manufacturer's instructions.
Makes 1 litre

CHOCOLATE ICE CREAM

750 mL (3 cups) milk
6 egg yolks (50 g)
200 g sugar
75 g cocoa powder

1   Make a custard base with the milk, eggs and sugar.
2   While the mixture is still hot, place the cocoa in a bowl and slowly whisk in the custard, a tablespoon at a time.
3   Chill, pour the mixture into your ice cream maker and freeze, following the manufacturer's instructions.
Makes 1 litre

Chocolate Ice Cream; Pistachio Ice Cream and Basic Vanilla Ice Cream made into a layered ice cream cake

CONTINENTAL CHOCOLATE ICE CREAM

600 mL milk
200 g sugar
6 egg yolks (60 g)
175 g dark cooking chocolate
250 mL (1 cup) cream

1 Make a custard base with the milk, sugar and egg yolks.
2 Break the chocolate into pieces and melt in a double boiler.
3 Place half the hot custard in a bowl and whisk in the chocolate quickly.
4 Return the chocolate custard to the custard on the stove and stir gently to incorporate.
5 Remove from heat, allow to cool and add the cream.
6 Place in ice cream maker and freeze, following the manufacturer's instructions.

VARIATIONS

MOKA FINE
Add 2 teaspoons instant coffee to custard.
CHOC RUM
Add 90 mL dark rum.
CHOC BRANDY
Add 90 mL brandy.
Makes 1 litre

COFFEE ICE CREAM

4 egg yolks (65 g)
100 g caster sugar
125 mL (½ cup) milk
125 mL (½ cup) cream
3 tablespoons instant coffee
  powder
1 teaspoon vanilla essence
500 mL (2 cups) cream

1 Place the egg yolks, sugar, milk, cream and coffee in a bowl over hot water.
2 Beat with a whisk for 10 minutes until thickened and doubled in volume.
3 Chill the mixture and add the cream.
4 Place the mixture in your ice cream maker and freeze, following the manufacturer's instructions.
Makes 1 litre

Coffee Ice Cream

ALMOND ICE CREAM

650 mL milk
150 g almonds, finely
  ground
200 g caster sugar
6 egg yolks (50 g)
200 mL cream

1 In a saucepan, heat the milk, almonds and 100 g sugar to boiling point, stirring constantly. Cover, remove from the heat and let stand for 10 minutes.
2 Place the egg yolks and remaining 100 g sugar in a bowl and beat until the mixture whitens and forms a ribbon.
3 Strain the almonds from the milk and bring the milk to the boil again. Pour a little boiling milk into the egg-sugar mix, whisking constantly.
4 Remove saucepan from the heat and pour egg-sugar mix into it, stirring constantly.
5 Return saucepan to a low heat, stirring constantly for 5–10 minutes until the mixture is thick.
6 Remove saucepan from heat and allow to cool in a bowl of iced water.
7 Add the cream, chill and then place the mixture in your ice cream maker and freeze, following the manufacturer's instructions.
Makes 1 litre

BUTTER PECAN NUT ICE CREAM

150 g pecan pieces
40 g unsalted butter
500 mL (2 cups) milk
350 mL cream
125 g brown sugar
1½ teaspoons vanilla essence
3 egg yolks (60 g)

1 Gently saute pecan pieces in butter until golden. Drain on paper towel.
2 Heat milk, cream, sugar and vanilla to simmering point, stirring to dissolve sugar.
3 Beat egg yolks until frothy, then whisk in small amount of warm milk.
4 Return the pan to heat and mix in eggs and milk. Cook over medium heat to thicken slightly, for about 7 minutes.
5 Chill for 25 minutes in refrigerator then add nuts.
6 Place the mixture in your ice cream maker and freeze, following the manufacturer's instructions.
Makes 1 litre

TOFFEE ICE CREAM

3 eggs (55 g)
3 egg yolks (55 g)
75 g sugar
600 mL milk
200 mL cream

CARAMEL
125 g (½ cup) sugar
200 mL water

1   Beat the eggs and yolks with the sugar until thick and creamy.
2   Heat the milk to boiling point and pour into the egg-sugar mix gradually, whisking all the time. Return to the heat in a saucepan and cook at low heat to thicken.
3   Chill in refrigerator.
4   Add 150 g caramel to chilled custard.
5   Add cream and freeze in your ice cream maker, following the manufacturer's instructions.

To make the caramel: Dissolve the sugar and 100 mL water in a heavy-based saucepan over a low heat, stirring occasionally. When it has melted, turn up the heat to boil the caramel into a rich syrup. Remove from the heat and carefully add the remaining water, stirring constantly. When cooled the caramel can be stored for later use in a screw-top jar.

Freezing Time Machine: 40 minutes — Hand: 3½ hours
Makes 1 litre

RICH HONEY ICE CREAM

100 mL milk
200 mL honey
6 egg yolks (50 g)
lemon juice, to taste
600 mL cream

1   Place the milk and honey in a saucepan and bring slowly to the boil, stirring constantly.
2   Whisk the egg yolks in a bowl until thick and light.
3   Whisk in the honey-milk mixture.
4   Return the mix to a rinsed pan over a low heat, whisking until thickened.
5   Remove and chill.
6   Add lemon juice and cream, and mix well.
7   Place the mixture in your ice cream maker and freeze, following the manufacturer's instructions.

Makes 1 litre

BANANA ICE CREAM

500 mL (2 cups) milk
150 g sugar
4 egg yolks (50 g)
650 g bananas, unpeeled
1½ tablespoons lemon juice

1   Make the custard with the milk, sugar and egg yolks and allow to cool.
2   When it is cold, peel the bananas and quickly puree with the lemon juice in a food processor.
3   Place the banana puree in a bowl and gradually add the custard, whisking constantly to obtain a smooth texture.
4   Transfer the mix to your tray or ice cream maker and freeze, following the manufacturer's instructions.

Note: The lemon juice will retard the banana browning only if the ice cream is kept out of contact with air, so place the mixture in an airtight container.
Makes 1 litre

KIWI FRUIT ICE CREAM

6 large kiwi fruit, peeled
175 g caster sugar
4 egg yolks (65 g)
125 mL (½ cup) milk
625 mL (2½ cups) cream
1 tablespoon vanilla essence

1   Puree kiwi fruit with 75 g sugar and allow to marinate for 2 hours in the refrigerator.
2   Beat the egg yolks, remaining 100 g sugar, milk, 125 mL (½ cup) cream and vanilla essence.
3   Set the bowl over a pan of hot water and beat until thickened and doubled in volume. Allow to cool.
4   Add 500 mL (2 cups) cream and chill.
5   Place mixture in your ice cream maker and freeze 20 minutes, following the manufacturer's instructions. Add fruit puree when the batch is half frozen and freeze another 20 minutes.

Note: The kiwi fruit will probably be dull in colour. To remedy this, use green food colouring or for something different, add Blue Curacao.
Makes 1 litre

Rich Honey Ice Cream

◇ MOUSSES, PARFAITS AND ◇ SOUFFLES

These iced desserts are light and airy, a perfect finish to a lunch or dinner party. They don't need an ice cream maker.

MOUSSES

These light-textured rich desserts are made with whisked egg yolks, whipped cream and sometimes egg whites or gelatine.

DAIQUIRI MOUSSE

5 eggs (60 g), separated
175 g caster sugar
100 mL lemon juice
grated rind 1½ lemons
1 tablespoon gelatine
60 mL white rum
225 mL cream, whipped

1   Whisk the egg yolks until light and fluffy. Gradually beat in 85 g sugar until dissolved, then whisk in the lemon juice and rind.

2   Place the bowl over a pan of hot water and cook gently like a custard until the mixture thickens.

3   Soak the gelatine in rum over a pan of hot water and when dissolved add to the egg mixture. Leave to cool.

4   Whisk the egg whites in a bowl until stiff and gradually add the remaining 90 g sugar.

5   When thoroughly beaten, fold the egg whites and the cream into the egg mix. Chill.

6   Place the mixture in a serving container and freeze.
Makes 1 litre

Moulded Daiquiri Mousse and scoops of Mainstay Pina Colada ice cream

1   *Whisk in lemon juice and rind*

2   *Heat gently until mixture thickens*

3   *Fold whisked egg whites into the egg mixture*

BUTTERSCOTCH MOUSSE

6 egg yolks
40 g unsalted butter
110 g brown sugar
225 mL hot water
450 mL cream, whipped

1   Place the egg yolks in a bowl and beat until thick and light.
2   In a heavy-based saucepan melt the butter and sugar. Bring to the boil and boil for 1 minute.
3   Carefully stir in the hot water and heat mixture to dissolve. While still hot, pour into the egg yolks, whisking all the time.
4   Clean the pan, pour the egg mix back in and continue to stir on a low heat until thick (do not boil).
5   Chill and then add cream.
6   Place the mixture in a serving container and freeze.
Makes 1 litre

APRICOT MOUSSE

75 g sugar
100 mL water
3 egg yolks (60 g)
550 g canned apricots,
    drained
75 g icing sugar
juice 1 lemon
300 mL cream

1   In a heavy saucepan boil the sugar and water, stirring occasionally until the temperature reaches 109°–112°C.
2   Whisk the egg yolks in a bowl until thick.
3   Slowly pour the hot syrup into the yolks whisking constantly until mixture is thick and light.
4   Puree the apricots with the icing sugar and lemon juice in a blender and fold the puree into the egg yolks.
5   Whisk the cream until thick and fold into puree. Place in container and freeze.
Note: If you do not have a sugar thermometer this temperature, 109°–112°C, is called the *blow* stage. To test this, slip a skimmer into the syrup then lift it out and blow hard through the holes — little bubbles of sugar will form (don't burn your mouth).
Makes 1 litre

THE ICED SOUFFLE

Add a syrup, flavouring and whipped cream to any leftover egg whites and you have the basis for a delicious souffle. Prepare a dish with a paper collar, then pile your mixture high in the manner of a cooked souffle.

ICED SOUFFLE (foundation recipe)

An iced souffle should resemble a baked souffle. To help you achieve this, create a collar around the dish, using non-stick baking paper. The collar should stand approximately 5 cm above the dish.

100 g sugar
140 mL water
pinch salt
2 egg whites (65 g)
250–275 mL fruit puree
150 mL cream, whipped

1   Heat sugar in the water until it dissolves; boil for 5 minutes.
2   Add salt to the egg whites and whisk until stiff. Pour hot syrup over them, whisking until thick.
3   Cool over ice, whisking occasionally.
4   Fold the fruit into the cream and add the egg white mix.
5   Chill, place mixture in a serving container and freeze. Do not beat after placing in freezer!
Makes approximately 500 mL

LEMON SOUFFLE

150 g sugar
250 mL (1 cup) water
grated rind 2 lemons
6 egg whites (65 g)
juice 4 lemons
275 mL cream, whipped

1   Boil the sugar, water, and lemon rind for 5 minutes.
2   Whisk the egg whites until stiff and pour the syrup over them, whisking until thick; allow to cool.
3   Add the lemon juice and fold in the cream.
4   Place mixture in a serving dish, freeze.
Makes 1 litre

1 Whisk egg whites in a bain marie until stiff

2 Fold in strawberry puree

3 Place in prepared souffle dish and freeze

Strawberry Souffle

STRAWBERRY SOUFFLE

175 g sugar
100 mL water
3 egg whites
300 mL cream, whipped
    and chilled
squeeze lemon juice, to taste
550 g strawberries, cleaned,
    hulled and pureed

1   Dissolve sugar in water, bring to boil and boil 5 minutes.
2   Whisk egg whites in a bain marie or double boiler until stiff.
3   Pour hot syrup onto egg whites slowly, whisking constantly.
4   Remove from heat, whisking to cool.
5   Fold in cream, lemon juice and strawberry puree.
6   Place mixture in a serving container and freeze.
Makes 1 litre

PARFAITS

Made with egg yolks and milk, similar to custard base ice creams, the parfait has a richer, lighter texture. It can be made in a serving dish such as a parfait glass or frozen in a shallow metal container and served in scoops.

GRAND MARNIER PARFAIT

200 mL Sugar Syrup I (see
    recipe)
4 egg yolks (50 g)
1½ tablespoons Grand
    Marnier
250 mL (1 cup) cream,
    whipped

1   Heat sugar syrup to lukewarm.
2   In a bowl beat the egg yolks well and slowly whisk in the syrup.
3   Place the egg-sugar mix in a double boiler over low heat for 20 minutes, stirring occasionally.
4   Remove pan from the heat and put the mixture in an electric mixer bowl. Beat on high speed 1 minute, medium speed 3 minutes and low speed 5 minutes.
5   Refrigerate 1 hour.
6   Gently fold in half the cream, add the Grand Marnier and the remainder of the cream.
7   Place the mixture in a serving container and freeze.
Makes 1 litre

STRAWBERRY PARFAIT

100 g granulated sugar
100 mL water
5 egg yolks (50 g)
300 g strawberries, cleaned,
    hulled and pureed
300 mL cream, whipped

1   In a small saucepan, heat sugar and water, stirring occasionally to dissolve. Bring to the boil and simmer.
2   Beat egg yolks until thick and creamy.
3   Slowly add the hot syrup, beating vigorously until light and fluffy.
4   Add the strawberry puree and fold in the whipped cream.
5   Place in a serving container and freeze.
Makes 1 litre

COFFEE PARFAIT

250 mL (1 cup) milk
200 g sugar
1½ teaspoons coarsely
    ground coffee
3 tablespoons instant coffee
6 egg yolks (50 g)
125 mL (½ cup) cream,
    whipped

1   In a saucepan heat the milk, 100 g sugar and the ground coffee. Bring to the boil. Cover and infuse for 10 minutes.
2   Strain the milk and add the instant coffee.
3   Beat the egg yolks and remaining 100 g sugar until the mixture whitens and forms a ribbon.
4   Bring the milk back to the boil and pour a little into the egg yolks, whisking constantly.
5   Return this mix to the milk and cook as for a custard, heating gently and stirring constantly for 10 minutes.
6   The custard must be beaten with an electric mixer (medium 5 minutes, slow 15 minutes) until cooled and thickened. The parfait should be nearly as thick as whipped cream or a sponge-cake batter.
7   Refrigerate for 1 hour and then gently and slowly fold in the whipped cream.
8   Place mixture in a serving container and freeze.
Makes 1 litre

MAPLE PECAN PARFAIT

100 g granulated sugar
90 mL maple syrup
6 egg yolks (50 g)
300 mL cream
100 g pecan nuts, lightly
    roasted and chopped

1   In a saucepan, combine sugar and maple syrup. Bring to boil, stirring constantly, to gradually dissolve sugar.
2   Whisk the egg yolks until thick and creamy.
3   Pour the hot syrup into the egg mix, beating constantly until thick and light.
4   Beat the cream until soft peaks form and fold into egg mix.
5   Add the nuts, place in a serving container and freeze 4–5 hours.
Makes 1 litre

1 Beat egg yolks and sugar to form a ribbon

2 Add chopped chocolate, a little at a time

3 Place mixture in a serving container such as a parfait glass and freeze

Chocolate Parfait

CHOCOLATE PARFAIT

250 mL (1 cup) milk
200 g sugar
6 egg yolks (50 g)
300 g plain chocolate,
  chopped
250 mL (1 cup) cream,
  whipped

1   Heat the milk with 100 g sugar and bring to boil.
2   Beat the egg yolks and remaining 100 g sugar to form a ribbon.
3   Pour a little hot milk into the egg yolks, whisking constantly. Pour back into the milk.
4   Cook gently for 10 minutes stirring constantly, then remove from heat.
5   Add chopped chocolate a little at a time.
6   Beat to cool in an electric mixer (medium 5 minutes, slow 15 minutes).
7   Chill 1 hour and add cream.
8   Place mixture in a serving container and freeze.
Makes 1 litre

31

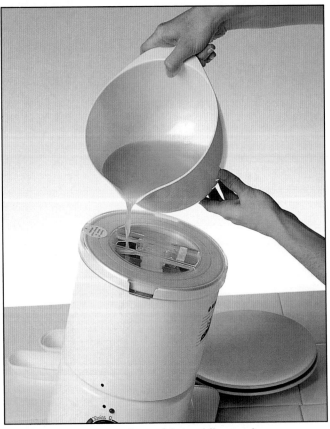

Orange Sorbet
1   *Combine orange juice and sugar syrup*

2   *Place in ice cream maker and freeze following the*
manufacturer's instructions

SORBETS AND SHERBETS

These are the traditional water ices so popular in hot Mediterranean climates. The basis for sorbet recipes is a sugar syrup, to which you can add a wonderful variety of ingredients, from rose petals to tomato and basil. With the addition of an egg white or cream and gelatine, sorbets become sherbets — light, fluffy, melt-in-the-mouth treats suitable for any occasion.

Gelato, loved the world over, is best described as a milk sherbet. Here we have two recipes for the favourite flavours — strawberry and chocolate!

Stir sorbets, sherbets and gelato recipes at least twice during freezing if you are making them by hand — after they are half-frozen and mushy, but before they become too hard. If you stir too soon they will simply turn back to liquid.

Any of the sorbet recipes can be made into sherbets by the addition of 1 egg white, as in the recipe for Lemon Sorbet/Sherbet.

SUGAR SYRUP I

This mixture is also useful in cocktail making and is known by the following names: bar syrup, simple syrup, gomme syrup and sugar syrup 28°. The 28° refers to the specific gravity of the solution as measured on a saccharometer.

1 kg granulated sugar
1 litre water

1 Place sugar and water in a heavy-based saucepan over high heat, stirring to dissolve. Continue heating until the mixture boils.

2   Remove from stove and, when the syrup has cooled, place in a covered container and refrigerate. This will keep for months.

Makes 1.5 litres

Lemon Sorbet and Orange Sorbet

QUICK SORBET (foundation recipe)

500–600 g fruit, pureed
500 mL Sugar Syrup I (see
recipe)

1 Blend together and freeze in your ice cream maker, following the manufacturer's instructions.
Makes 1 litre

ORANGE SORBET

550 mL orange juice,
strained
420 mL Sugar Syrup I (see
recipe)

1 Combine orange juice and sugar syrup.
2 Refrigerate until chilled.
3 Place in ice cream maker and churn, following the manufacturer's instructions.
Serving Suggestions: Use as an accompaniment to a fresh fruit platter.
Makes 1 litre

LEMON SORBET/SHERBET

250 mL (1 cup) lemon juice,   *325 mL Sugar Syrup I (see*
strained   *recipe)*
200 mL water   *1 egg white (65 g) (for*
sherbet)

1 Combine lemon juice, water and sugar syrup and place in ice cream maker.
2 Churn for 25 minutes and then stop the machine.
3 Place 2 tablespoons of mixture in a bowl with the egg white. Whisk vigorously until mixture is thick and foamy.
4 Pour back into the machine and finish freezing.
Serving Suggestion: To serve in the lemon skins, cut the top section off the lemons and spoon out the flesh. Push it through a sieve to give the juice for the sorbet. Freeze skins. When the ice is churned, brush the skins with sugar syrup and turn them upside down to drain. Then pipe the ice into the skin containers with a large decorative nozzle. Replace the top at an angle.
Makes 1 litre

MELON SORBET

This recipe is for those unable to eat sucrose (ordinary cane sugar) so honey has been substituted.

100 mL honey
200 mL water
1.5 kg rockmelon, seeded
    and chopped
1 teaspoon ginger
100 mL lemon juice

1   Gently dissolve the honey in water in a saucepan.
2   Pulp the melon in a blender with the ginger and cooled honey.
3   Add lemon juice to taste and chill for 30 minutes.
4   Place the mixture in your ice cream maker and freeze, following the manufacturer's instructions.
Makes 1 litre

ROSE PETAL SORBET

To prepare the rose petals for this recipe, remove the individual petals gently and discard the stamens and hips. Be careful of dusting powders that are often used on rose bushes. If you are not sure about insecticides then wash the whole flower before you begin to make the sorbet. The colour of roses used will affect the final result: a combination of red and white petals will produce a mauve sorbet.

750 g (3 cups) sugar
750 mL (3 cups) water
750 mL (3 cups) firmly
    packed rose petals
400 mL water
1 egg white

1   Combine the sugar and 750 mL water in a saucepan, stirring occasionally to dissolve.
2   Place rose petals in hot syrup and cover saucepan. Reduce heat and simmer for 15 minutes, shaking pan occasionally.
3   Remove from heat and when cool, place in refrigerator and leave overnight.
4   The following day, strain the syrup and add 400 mL water. Discard the rose petals.
5   Place mixture in your ice cream maker and process for approximately 15 minutes, following the manufacturer's instructions.
6   Add 1 egg white, beaten till soft peaks form.
7   Return to your ice cream maker and continue churning until frozen, approximately 15 minutes.
Makes 2 litres

PEPINO SORBET

The pepino, originally from South America, is known as the melon bush. Related to the tomato, this fruit is golden with purple stripes and tastes a little like rockmelon and honeydew.

While small and green, pepino can be prepared like zucchini or used in relishes, chutneys and cakes. The larger green variety is ideal as a salad vegetable.

500 g pepinos, cleaned and
    cored
400 mL (2 cups) Sugar
    Syrup I (see recipe)
75 mL lemon juice
½ teaspoon ginger, to taste

1   In a blender, combine the pepino, sugar syrup and lemon juice at high speed until smooth.
2   Sprinkle in ginger.
3   Place mixture in your ice cream maker and freeze for approximately 30 minutes, following the manufacturer's instructions.
Makes 1 litre

STRAWBERRY SORBET

600 g fresh strawberries,
    washed, hulled and
    pureed
400 mL cold Sugar Syrup I
    (see recipe)
1–2 tablespoons lemon juice

1   Combine all ingredients.
2   Place in your ice cream maker and freeze, following the manufacturer's instructions.
Makes 1 litre

Rose Petal Sorbet

Mango and Kiwi Fruit Sorbet

MANGO AND KIWI FRUIT SORBET

1 ripe mango, peeled, stoned
  and sliced
6 kiwi fruit, peeled and
  sliced
315 mL (1¼ cups) Sugar
  Syrup I (see recipe)

1 tablespoon orange juice
extra fruit, for garnish
  (optional)

1   Puree the mango and kiwi fruit in a food processor. Add sugar syrup and orange juice. Blend well.

2   Pour mixture into ice cream maker and freeze, following the manufacturer's instructions.

3   Just before serving, spoon into chilled glasses with extra slices of fruit for garnish.

Serves 4

MANGO SORBET

65 g sugar
2 mangoes peeled, seeded
  and pureed
65 mL orange juice

80 mL water
2 teaspoons lemon juice
2 egg whites

1   In a saucepan, combine sugar and mango puree. Bring to boil, stirring constantly. Cover and simmer for 5 minutes.

2   Remove mixture from heat. Add orange juice, water, lemon juice and mix well. Cool slightly.

3   Pour mixture into a 30 × 20 cm plastic container. Place in freezer until mixture is thick but not set.

4   Whisk egg whites until stiff peaks form. Beat mango mixture until light and frothy, then fold into egg whites.

5   Freeze until firm.

Note: Canned mangoes can also be used in this recipe.

Serves 6

THE SAVOURY SORBET

AVOCADO SORBET

*1 kg ripe avocados, peeled
  and seeded
200 mL lemon juice
400 mL Sugar Syrup I (see
  recipe)*

1   Peel and seed avocados and place in blender with lemon juice; blend at high speed.

2   Slowly add sugar syrup and continue blending until you have a smooth consistency.

3   Adjust taste with lemon juice.

4   Place in your ice cream maker and freeze, following the manufacturer's instructions.

Makes 1 litre

TOMATO AND BASIL SORBET

*1 kg ripe tomatoes
125 mL (½ cup) lemon juice
125 mL (½ cup) Sugar Syrup
  I (see recipe)
1 teaspoon salt
1 tablespoon tomato paste
6 leaves basil, coarsely
  chopped*

1   Plunge tomatoes in boiling water for 30–60 seconds and peel skin.

2   Remove the seeds and puree tomatoes in a blender.

3   Place the puree in a bowl and combine with remaining ingredients.

4   Chill for 30 minutes in refrigerator.

5   Place the mixture in your ice cream maker and freeze, following the manufacturer's instructions.

Makes 1 litre

Avocado Sorbet and Tomato and Basil Sorbet

GELATO

STRAWBERRY GELATO

500 mL (2 cups) milk
175 g sugar
125 g skim milk powder
400 g strawberries, washed,
 hulled and pureed
1 tablespoon lemon juice
1½ teaspoons vanilla essence

1 Gently heat the milk, sugar and skim milk powder until dissolved.

2 Chill 30 minutes.

3 Stir in strawberries, lemon juice and vanilla.

4 Mix thoroughly, place in your ice cream maker and freeze, following the manufacturer's instructions.

Makes 1 litre

CHOCOLATE GELATO

750 mL (3 cups) milk
250 g sugar
125 g unsweetened cooking
 chocolate

1 Heat the milk and sugar gently in a saucepan until the sugar is dissolved.

2 In another pan melt the chocolate slowly on low heat.

3 When smooth gradually add the sweetened milk, stirring constantly. Cook over medium heat until well combined.

4 Chill in refrigerator and then place the mixture in your ice cream maker and freeze, following the manufacturer's instructions.

Note: A low calorie version of this can be made by substituting skim milk for full cream milk.

Makes 1 litre

Chocolate Gelato and Strawberry Gelato

GRANITAS

Granita, gramolata, granulated or slush ice is an iced drink resembling a sorbet, served as a sweet or refreshment at parties.

Prepare granita in a shallow metal tray and freeze without stirring. To serve, draw the serving spoon across the surface to produce a granula ice.

SUGAR SYRUP II

250 g (1 cup) sugar
500 mL (2 cups) water

1 Place ingredients in a saucepan over medium heat and stir occasionally to dissolve.
2 Bring to the boil, simmer for 2 minutes, then remove from heat and cool.
Note: This syrup is also known as Sugar Syrup 14°, which refers to the specific gravity of the solution as measured on a saccharometer.

BASIC GRANITA RECIPE

750 mL (3 cups) fruit puree
  or pulp
250 mL (1 cup) Sugar Syrup
  II (see recipe)

1 Combine fruit puree and sugar syrup and mix well.
2 Pour into a shallow metal tray and freeze without stirring or churning. Do not scoop — draw the serving spoon across the surface to produce a granular ice.

STRAWBERRY AND REDCURRANT GRANITA

500 g strawberries
250 g redcurrants
250 mL (1 cup) Sugar Syrup
  II (see recipe)
juice 1 lemon

1 Wash and hull strawberries.
2 Remove stalks from redcurrants and wash.
3 Puree berries in blender at high speed for 30 seconds, slowly adding sugar syrup.
4 Add lemon juice, pour into a shallow tray and freeze 2–3 hours.
Makes 1 litre

LEMON GRANITA

6 lemons
750 mL (3 cups) lemon juice
250 mL (1 cup) Sugar Syrup
  II (see recipe)

1 Before squeezing lemons, finely grate the rind of 6 lemons and reserve the zest.
2 Make a sugar syrup, add zest and chill.
3 Combine juice and sugar syrup in shallow metal tray and place in freezer. Stir every hour to prevent separation of the juice and syrup. Freeze 3 hours.
4 Serve in scooped out lemon skins that have been dipped in sugar syrup and refrigerated.
Makes 1 litre

ALMOND GRANITA

250 g almonds
250 g (1 cup) sugar
500 mL (2 cups) water

1 Place almonds in shallow baking dish under a hot grill and 'roast' for 10 minutes, shaking the dish occasionally.
2 Remove the nuts and grind coarsely in a food processor.
3 Place the sugar, water and nuts in a saucepan and heat gently to dissolve the sugar. Bring to the boil, stirring occasionally, and simmer for 5 minutes.
4 Remove from heat, cool and place in refrigerator overnight.
5 On the following day, strain the syrup, pour it into a shallow metal dish and freeze 2–3 hours.
Makes 1 litre

WATERMELON GRANITA

2 kg watermelon
juice ½ orange
500 mL (2 cups) Sugar
    Syrup II (see recipe)

1   Peel and seed the watermelon and chop the flesh.
2   Puree in a blender with orange juice and sugar syrup.
3   Pour into a shallow metal dish and place in the freezer 2–3 hours or use an ice cream maker, following the manufacturer's instructions.
4   Serve in half rockmelon shells that have been dipped in sugar syrup and refrigerated.

Makes 1 litre

PINEAPPLE GRANITA

1.8 kg pineapple
juice 1 lemon
juice 1 orange
300 mL Sugar Syrup II (see
    recipe)

1   Cut pineapple top off at two-thirds height and remove flesh without breaking shell. Discard core and chop flesh to yield approximately 900 g fruit.
2   Puree pineapple in blender with citrus juices and sugar syrup at high speed for 30 seconds.
3   Pour into a shallow metal dish and place in the freezer 2–3 hours.
4   Serve in the pineapple shell.

Makes 1 litre

SOUR CHERRY GRANITA

750 g sour cherries, cleaned
    and stoned
juice ½ lemon
juice ½ orange
60 mL maraschino
200 mL Sugar Syrup II (see
    recipe)

1   Place cherries, citrus juices and liqueur in bowl and macerate overnight in refrigerator.
2   Place bowl contents in blender and puree on high speed for 30 seconds.
3   Strain pulp through sieve and add sugar syrup.
4   Place in shallow metal container and freeze 2–3 hours.

Makes 1 litre

CHAMPAGNE GRANITA WITH SUMMER BERRY FRUIT

500 mL brut champagne
300 mL maraschino
350 mL Sugar Syrup II (see
    recipe)
raspberries, strawberries,
    blackberries or
    blueberries

1   Mix champagne, 150 mL maraschino and sugar syrup together and freeze 2–3 hours in a shallow metal dish, stirring occasionally every hour.
2   Clean and wash berries, cut strawberries in halves or quarters, sprinkle wth maraschino and refrigerate until granita is frozen.
3   Scoop granita into serving dish alternating with fruit. Top with fruit and drizzle over small amount of juice.

Makes 1 litre

From top left clockwise: three refreshing granitas — Sour Cherry, Pineapple and Watermelon

YOGHURT ICE CREAMS

Yoghurt is one of nature's gifts to us. A good source of protein, it also produces bacteria beneficial to the digestive system, replacing normal intestinal bacteria killed off by antibiotics. Use on its own or blended with milk, cream or soft cheeses. Fat-reduced yoghurts should have gelatine or whisked egg white to soften the texture.

From top clockwise: Apple Yoghurt Ice; Low Cal Fruit Yoghurt Ice and Natural Muesli Ice Cream

APPLE YOGHURT ICE

700 g green cooking apples, cored and sliced	150 g granulated sugar
¼ teaspoon nutmeg	2 oranges
¼ teaspoon cinnamon	500 mL (2 cups) plain yoghurt

1   Place apples in saucepan with spices and sugar.

2   Add the grated rind of 1 orange and the juice of both to the apples.

3   Bring to the boil gradually and simmer until soft.

4   Cool, blend and sieve.

5   Add yoghurt and place the mixture in your ice cream maker. Freeze, following the manufacturer's instructions.

Makes 1 litre

NATURAL MUESLI ICE CREAM

200 g raw sugar
250 mL (1 cup) water
400 mL plain yoghurt
250 mL (1 cup) cream

HOMEMADE MUESLI

200 g mixed grains —
    wheatmeal, wheat flakes,
    oat flakes, maize meal,
    rye flakes and bran
2 tablespoons chopped
    hazelnuts, almonds and
    walnuts
2 tablespoons raisins
2 tablespoons chopped dried
    apples or apricots
2 tablespoons brown sugar

1   Dissolve the sugar in 250 mL (1 cup) water, and bring to the boil, stirring slowly. Simmer for 5 minutes; cool.
2   Combine with the yoghurt, cream and homemade muesli.
3   Place mixture in your ice cream maker and freeze, following the manufacturer's instructions.

Makes 1 litre

BLUEBERRY YOGHURT ICE

165 mL honey
100 mL water
300 g blueberries
400 mL plain yoghurt

1   Dissolve the honey in water in a saucepan over moderate heat.
2   Pour the syrup over the berries and lightly crush the fruit.
3   Place mixture in refrigerator overnight.
4   The following day, blend the mixture and sieve to remove skins.
5   Mix in yoghurt and place in your ice cream maker. Freeze, following manufacturer's instructions.

Makes 1 litre

LOW CAL FRUIT YOGHURT ICE

500 mL (2 cups) low-fat
    yoghurt
1 tablespoon lemon juice
apple juice concentrate, to
    taste
250 mL (1 cup) orange juice
4 egg whites
2 tablespoons skim milk
    powder

2 cups diced apple, orange,
    melon, pineapple or
    strawberry

1   Combine the yoghurt, lemon juice and apple juice concentrate.
2   Blend the orange juice and skim milk powder and add to yoghurt.
3   Whisk the egg whites and fold into the mixture.
4   Place the mixture in your ice cream maker and freeze, following the manufacturer's instructions.
5   Before serving, add diced fruit and combine well.

Makes 1 litre

RASPBERRY YOGHURT ICE

400 g raspberries
250 mL Sugar Syrup II (see
    recipe)
300 mL plain yoghurt
30 mL lemon juice

1   Puree raspberries with sugar syrup in a blender on high speed for 15 seconds.
2   Pour contents into a bowl and beat in yoghurt and lemon juice.
3   Place in your ice cream maker and freeze, following the manufacturer's instructions.

Makes 1 litre

YOGHURT HONEY ICE

150 mL honey
6 egg yolks (60 g)
700 mL yoghurt

1   Heat the honey on low heat to almost boiling.
2   Whisk the egg yolks until pale and frothy.
3   Beat in the honey gradually and continue beating until cool.
4   Whisk in yoghurt and place mixture in your ice cream maker. Freeze, following the manufacturer's instructions.

Makes 1 litre

PRITIKIN STYLE DIET

The absence of fat, salt and sugar in an ice cream certainly makes it difficult to manufacture as a hard ice cream.

The following recipes, however, are suitable not only for consumption straight out of the machine, but can be successfully frozen and served at a later date.

While the Pritikin regimen does not allow refined sugar — white, brown, honey, molasses or fructose — concentrated apple juice and grape juice are allowed in small quantities. These have some natural sugar also and are not recommended as a beverage, only as a recipe sweetener.

The diet also allows non-fat milk, up to 1% by weight or the equivalent in powdered skim milk.

PRITIKIN STYLE MANGO ICE CREAM

1 tablespoon gelatine
500 mL mango pulp
375 g unsweetened
   evaporated skim milk
1 teaspoon vanilla essence
30 mL apple juice
   concentrate
2 tablespoons skim milk
   powder

1   Dissolve the gelatine in a small amount of warm water.
2   Add to the other ingredients and blend until smooth.
3   Place the mixture in your ice cream maker and freeze, following the manufacturer's instructions.
Makes 1 litre

PRITIKIN STYLE RASPBERRY SORBET

500 g raspberries
350 mL apple juice
160 mL apple juice
   concentrate

1   Puree raspberries with apple juice on medium speed in blender for 15 seconds.
2   Place in your ice cream maker, add apple juice concentrate and freeze, following the manufacturer's instructions.
Makes 1 litre

PRITIKIN STYLE MINT AND APPLE SORBET

400 mL apple juice
4 cups mint leaves
½ teaspoon gelatine
200 mL apple juice
   concentrate
300 mL lemon juice
1 egg white

1   Bring the apple juice to the boil and pour onto the mint.
2   Place in refrigerator overnight to infuse.
3   Dissolve the gelatine in a small quantity of water.
4   Strain the mint and add gelatine, apple juice concentrate, and lemon juice to the liquid.
5   Place mixture in your ice cream maker and freeze for 15 minutes.
6   Beat egg white, add to mixture, return to ice cream maker and freeze again for another 15 minutes.
Makes 1 litre

PRITIKIN STYLE APPLE SORBET

400 g cooked diced apple (no
   added sugar)
160 mL apple juice
   concentrate
330 mL apple juice
100 mL lemon juice

1   Puree diced apple with apple juice concentrate in blender on high speed for 30 seconds.
2   Reduce speed to medium and add apple and lemon juices.
3   Place mixture in your ice cream maker and freeze, following the manufacturer's instructions, to make ice cream as solid as possible.
Makes 1 litre

PRITIKIN STYLE STRAWBERRY SORBET

350 g strawberries, washed
*   and hulled*
160 mL apple juice
*   concentrate*
300 mL apple juice
60 mL lemon juice

1   Place berries and apple juice concentrate in blender and process at high speed for 30 seconds.

2   Slow the blender to medium and add apple and lemon juices.

3   Place in your ice cream maker and freeze, following the manufacturer's instructions.

Makes approximately 1 litre

PRITIKIN STYLE APRICOT ICE

1½ tablespoons gelatine
500 g dried apricots, soaked
*   in water overnight*
375 mL (1½ cups) low-fat
*   evaporated skim milk*
1 teaspoon vanilla essence
125 mL (½ cup) apple juice
*   concentrate*

1   Dissolve gelatine in small amount of hot water.

2   Add to other ingredients and blend.

3   Pour into your ice cream maker and freeze, following the manufacturer's instructions.

Makes 1.5 litres

From top clockwise: Pritikin style iced desserts — Raspberry Sorbet; Mango Ice Cream and Mint and Apple Sorbet

OTHER ALTERNATIVES

Useful for vegetarians or experimental cooks, try soya milk, carob and tofu. Soya milk is ideal, low calorie, cholesterol-free form of milk with a 'beany' flavour which can be avoided by using a powdered soy. Carob is a flavouring from the locust bean, originating in the Middle East. It is often used as an alternative to chocolate. Tofu is unfermented bean curd, high in protein, low in calories and fat, and cholesterol-free. Try the finer imported Silken Tofu, available from health food and Asian food stores.

ORANGE MANGO TOFU ICE

2 teaspoons gelatine
350 mL orange mango juice
   concentrate
250 g tofu
1½ teaspoons lecithin
   (preferably liquid)
100 mL plain vegetable oil
180 g honey
180 mL glucose or corn
   syrup

1   Dissolve gelatine in a little water.
2   Blend remaining ingredients together until smooth.
3   Add gelatine, place mixture in your ice cream maker and freeze, following the manufacturer's instructions.
Makes 1 litre

CAROB AND BANANA ICE

450 g fresh tofu
225 mL soya milk, fresh or
   powdered
100 mL vegetable oil
120 g brown sugar
120 g banana, peeled
3 tablespoons carob powder
   or *syrup*

1   Break up the tofu.
2   Blend all ingredients together in several batches until smooth.
3   Place mixture in your ice cream maker and freeze, following the manufacturer's instructions.
Note: Low-fat and high water content in this ice makes it freeze very solid. Remove from the freezer 30 minutes prior to serving and allow to sit at room temperature.
Makes 1 litre

TOFU PEACH PARFAIT

1.2 kg peaches, fresh or   150 mL glucose or corn
   canned and drained   syrup
350 mL apple juice   500 g tofu (silken preferably)
   concentrate   pinch cinnamon
2 teaspoons gelatine   pinch ginger

1   Blend peaches and apple juice concentrate at high speed in blender for 30 seconds.
2   Dissolve the gelatine in a small quantity of water and add to the glucose.
3   Blend the tofu and peaches at high speed for 30 seconds.
4   In a bowl combine all ingredients, whisking them together. Pour into parfait glasses.
5   Refrigerate for 3 hours but *do not freeze*.
Makes 2 litres

PEANUT BUTTER TOFU

400 g crunchy peanut butter
100 mL walnut oil
250 g tofu
100 mL soya milk
150 g brown sugar
100 mL glucose
2 teaspoons gelatine,
   dissolved in small amount
   of water

1   Blend all ingredients together in several batches.
2   Place mixture in your ice cream maker and freeze, according to the manufacturer's instructions.
Makes 1 litre

SOYA PINA COLADA

250 mL drained canned
   pineapple
250 mL honey
juice 1 orange
lemon juice, to taste
250 mL (1 cup) soya milk
250 mL (1 cup) coconut milk

1   Place all ingredients in blender and process until smooth.
2   Pour into your ice cream maker and freeze, following the manufacturer's instructions.
Makes 1 litre

Alternative iced desserts: Peanut Butter Tofu; Tofu Peach Parfait and Soya Pina Colada

◇ OLD TIME FAVOURITES ◇

JUST AS GRANDMA MADE IT!

These delicious old-time favourites were especially selected from an original ice cream book first used by our grandmothers to make ice cream at home with farm fresh ingredients.

The recipes came with the manual for the early kerosene fridges which were imported from Sweden and later manufactured in Australia by Electrolux in the mid 1930s. Freezing compartments were fitted with one small tray, so the recipes make only small quantities. Electrolux, now more famous for its vacuum cleaners, still makes small caravan gas/electric fridges and these recipes would be ideal to use on holidays, especially when you don't have your ice cream machine or other standard kitchen equipment with you.

These ice creams, reproduced courtesy of Electrolux, can be simply made with a hand beater. Be careful not to over whip the cream so it's not too stiff, and fold in the other ingredients slowly and carefully. The careful folding-in process preserves the air bubbles in the whipped cream to make a creamy smooth ice cream.

BETTY'S FAVOURITE ICE CREAM

200 mL sweetened
  condensed milk
600 mL lukewarm milk
4 tablespoons powdered full
  cream milk
pinch salt
2 teaspoons gelatine
125 mL (½ cup) warm
  water
vanilla essence, to taste

1   In a bowl, combine condensed milk, warm milk, powdered milk and salt. Beat till powdered milk dissolves.

2   Dissolve gelatine in ½ cup warm water and add to mixture. Beat again and add vanilla. Beat once more.

3   Pour mixture into metal dish and freeze. When partly set, tip into basin and beat until smooth again with fork. Return to dish and complete freezing.
Makes 600 mL

CHOCOLATE MINT ICE CREAM

1 tablespoon cocoa
125 mL (½ cup) water
65 mL (¼ cup) milk
pinch salt
90 g sugar

½ teaspoon vanilla essence
few drops peppermint
  essence
250 mL (1 cup) cream,
  whipped

1   Combine cocoa and water in the top of a double boiler and heat until mixed.

2   Add milk, salt and sugar. When sugar is dissolved, remove from heat and allow to cool.

3   Add essences and fold the mixture slowly into the whipped cream.

4   Pour into shallow metal dish and freeze to desired consistency.
Makes 500 mL

TOASTED COCONUT ICE CREAM

60 g sugar
pinch salt
65 mL (¼ cup) milk
1 teaspoon vanilla essence
20 g shredded coconut,
  toasted
250 mL (1 cup) cream,
  whipped

1   Combine first 5 ingredients and fold slowly into whipped cream.

2   Pour the mixture into a shallow metal dish and freeze to the desired consistency.
Makes 400 mL

PEACH ICE CREAM

125 mL (1 cup) pureed
  peaches
125 g (½ cup) sugar
pinch salt
65 mL (¼ cup) milk
250 mL (1 cup) cream,
  whipped

1   Combine first 4 ingredients, stir, and fold slowly into whipped cream.

2   Pour the mixture into a shallow metal dish and freeze to the desired consistency.
Makes 500 mL

From top clockwise: Chocolate Mint Ice Cream; Toasted Coconut Ice Cream and Betty's Favourite Ice Cream

RASPBERRY ICE CREAM

250 g raspberries
125 g (½ cup) sugar
pinch salt
65 mL (¼ cup) milk
250 mL (1 cup) cream,
  whipped

1   Combine raspberries, sugar, salt and milk. Fold slowly into whipped cream.
2   Pour mixture into a shallow metal dish and freeze to the desired consistency.
Makes 500 mL

CARROT ICE CREAM

125 mL (½ cup) pureed
  cooked carrot
85 mL carrot juice
90 g brown sugar
2 tablespoons milk
½ teaspoon vanilla essence
pinch salt
pinch each nutmeg, cloves
  and cinnamon
190 mL (¾ cup) cream,
  whipped

1   Combine carrot puree and juice with sugar, milk, vanilla and salt. Add spices and stir thoroughly.
2   Fold the mixture slowly into whipped cream.
3   Pour the mixture into a shallow metal dish and freeze to the desired consistency.
Makes 500 mL

PUMPKIN ICE CREAM

125 mL (½ cup) cooked
  mashed pumpkin
65 mL (¼ cup) milk
50 g brown sugar
pinch salt
½ teaspoon cinnamon
¼ teaspoon ginger
½ teaspoon vanilla essence
250 mL (1 cup) cream,
  whipped

1   Combine all ingredients except cream.
2   Fold the mixture slowly into whipped cream.
3   Pour into a shallow metal dish and freeze to the desired consistency.
Makes 500 mL

CHOCOLATE MARLOW

2 teaspoons cocoa powder
125 mL (½ cup) water
125 mL (½ cup) scalded
  milk
20 marshmallows
pinch salt
1 teaspoon vanilla essence
250 mL (1 cup) cream,
  whipped

1   Combine cocoa with water in the top of a double boiler. Heat until mixed and smooth.
2   Add scalded milk and 15 marshmallows. Stir and continue cooking until marshmallows are dissolved.
3   Remove from heat and chill until slightly thickened. Add salt and vanilla.
4   Cut the remaining 5 marshmallows into small pieces and add to whipped cream.
5   Fold the first mixture slowly into the whipped cream.
6   Pour the complete mixture into a shallow metal dish and freeze to desired consistency.
Makes 500 mL

NUT PARFAIT

125 g (½ cup) sugar
65 mL water
2 egg whites (65 g)
½ teaspoon vanilla essence
60 g walnuts, chopped
crystallised pineapple or
  glace cherries, chopped
250 mL (1 cup) cream,
  whipped
glace cherries, for garnish

1   Combine sugar and water in saucepan and boil until it spins a thread.
2   Beat egg whites until stiff, add syrup gradually and beat until cool.
3   Add vanilla and fold in nuts, crystallised pineapple and whipped cream.
4   Place mixture in a shallow metal dish and freeze to desired consistency.
5   Serve garnished with cherries.
Makes 500 mL

Chocolate Marlow (above) and Nut Parfait (below)

PEANUT BRITTLE ICE CREAM

125 mL (½ cup) finely
   crushed peanut brittle
½ teaspoon vanilla essence
pinch salt
65 mL (¼ cup) milk
250 mL (1 cup) cream,
   whipped

1   Combine the first 4 ingredients and stir until the brittle is thoroughly dissolved.
2   Fold the mixture slowly into the whipped cream.
3   Pour into a shallow metal dish and freeze to the desired consistency.
Makes 450 mL

BURNT ALMOND ICE CREAM

60 g sugar
pinch salt
65 mL (¼ cup) milk
1 teaspoon almond essence
½ teaspoon vanilla essence
50 g almonds, blanched,
   chopped and toasted
250 mL (1 cup) cream,
   whipped

1   Combine all ingredients except cream.
2   Fold slowly into whipped cream.
3   Pour mixture into a shallow metal dish and freeze to the desired consistency.
Makes approximately 500 mL

PINEAPPLE SHERBET

20 marshmallows
250 mL (1 cup) unsweetened
   pineapple juice
85 mL (⅓ cup) water
2 tablespoons lemon juice
2 teaspoons sugar
pinch salt
2 egg whites, beaten (65 g)

1   Combine marshmallows, pineapple juice and water in top of double boiler and heat until marshmallows are melted; cool.
2   Add lemon juice and 1 teaspoon sugar. Pour mixture into a shallow metal dish and freeze to a mush.
3   Combine remaining sugar, salt and stiffly beaten egg whites.
4   Stir the partly frozen sherbet into this mixture and return to freezer. Stir again when mixture has frozen to a mush; then freeze to desired consistency.
Makes approximately 500 mL

FROZEN STRAWBERRY WHIP

250 g strawberries
185 g sugar
190 mL (¾ cup) water
½ teaspoon baking powder
pinch salt
2 egg whites, beaten (65 g)
250 mL (1 cup) cream,
   whipped

1   Wash, hull and puree strawberries, reserving a few for garnish.
2   Combine sugar, water, baking powder and salt in a saucepan. Cook until it spins a thread.
3   Pour mixture slowly over stiffly beaten egg whites and beat until cool.
4   Fold in strawberries and cream.
5   Pour mixture into shallow metal dish and freeze to desired consistency.
6   Serve in tall glasses garnished with a few strawberries.
Makes 500 mL

FROZEN CARAMEL

1 tablespoon cornflour
250 mL (1 cup) milk
125 mL (½ cup) glucose or
   corn syrup
125 g sugar
½ teaspoon vanilla essence
125 mL (½ cup) cream,
   whipped

1   Moisten cornflour with a little milk. Scald remaining milk and add glucose and moistened cornflour. Cook in top of a double boiler for about 10 minutes, stirring well.
2   Caramelise sugar in a shallow pan on the heat and stir constantly until sugar liquefies like toffee.
3   Add caramelised sugar gradually to hot milk mixture. Continue cooking and stir until well blended.
4   Cool and add vanilla. Fold into whipped cream.
5   Pour the mixture into a shallow metal dish and freeze to desired consistency.
Makes 500 mL

FROZEN FRUIT SALAD

60 g cream cheese
65 mL (¼ cup) mayonnaise
2 teaspoons lemon juice
¼ teaspoon salt

170 mL drained crushed
  pineapple
85 mL maraschino cherries
125 mL (½ cup) cream,
  whipped

1   Blend cream cheese and mayonnaise.
2   Add lemon juice, salt and fruit.
3   Fold in whipped cream.
4   Place mixture in a shallow metal dish and freeze to desired consistency.
Serving Suggestion: Serve sliced on lettuce with fresh fruit sauce.
Makes 500 mL

CHERRY MOSS

1 tablespoon gelatine
2 tablespoons cold water
225 mL hot water
250 mL dark red canned or
  stewed cherries, drained,
  pitted and halved

225 mL cherry juice
2 egg whites, beaten (65 g)
whipped cream and
  walnuts, for garnish

1   Soak gelatine in cold water and then dissolve in hot water.
2   Add cherries and cherry juice.
3   When mixture begins to thicken, beat; add beaten egg whites and mix thoroughly.
4   Turn the mixture into a lightly oiled mould and chill in refrigerator.
5   Unmould, garnish with whipped cream and sprinkle thickly with chopped walnuts.
Makes 750 mL

Cherry Moss (above) and Frozen Fruit Salad (below)

CHILD'S PLAY

Whatever your age, you can always experiment with new and exciting ice cream. Sweets for the young and sweet-toothed, ice cream cakes for birthdays and celebrations, and delicious alcoholic confections for festive occasions, all give a chef the chance to expand the family repertoire.

ICE CREAM CAKE

1 litre each 3 different
  flavoured ice creams

FROSTING
130 g dark cooking chocolate
175 mL condensed milk
250 mL (1 cup) whipping
  cream

1   Line a 5 litre container with non-stick baking paper.
2   Pour in 1 flavour of ice cream and allow to freeze for a minimum of 5 hours before pouring in the next layer of different flavoured ice cream. Freeze for a further 5 hours.
3   Repeat with third layer and freeze for 5 hours again.
4   Unmould, remove paper and carve into the required shape eg. heart, round, football, boat etc. (Remaining ice cream can be scooped up with a melon baller and used to decorate cake or returned to freezer.)
5   Heat chocolate and condensed milk in a pan, stirring occasionally.
6   Cool, then chill in refrigerator.
7   Whisk cream until stiff, whisk into chocolate and place in freezer for 30 minutes.
8   Spread or pipe frosting onto ice cream cake and serve.

NUMBER CAKE

To celebrate a birthday try an ice cream cake in the shape of the number of the birthday or year you are celebrating.

3 litres ice cream

1   Have a cake board or tray big enough to take 2 blocks of ice cream across and 6 along its length (each block being 500 mL).
2   Soften the ice cream by leaving it for 30 minutes in the refrigerator.
3   With a palette knife dipped in hot water, smooth the sides of the iced blocks and push together. Smooth the top and outsides of the total mass.
4   Freeze for 30 minutes.
5   Etch the shape of the number required on the block. Dip the knife in hot water again and cut the figure out.
6   Smooth over the figure and return to freezer.
7   Soften the leftover ice cream and place back in a container.
Serving Suggestions: Decorate with whipped cream and fresh fruit; cover with meringue as for Bombe Alaska (*see recipe*) and bake 3–5 minutes; coat with chocolate.
Serves 8

BANANA AND YOGHURT POPSICLES

150 mL honey
4 large bananas
300 mL low-fat yoghurt

1   Heat the honey briefly in a saucepan.
2   Combine the bananas and yoghurt in a blender until smooth.
3   Continue blending and add the honey gradually.
4   Pour into popsicle moulds and freeze.
Makes 1 litre

Serving suggestions for a children's party: Number Cake, colourful scoops and sundae faces

CANADIAN FREEZE

250 mL (1 cup) milk
100 mL maple syrup
250 mL (1 cup) cream

1 Heat the milk over a low heat.
2 Add the maple syrup, stirring to dissolve.
3 Cool and add the cream.
4 Pour into lolly moulds and freeze.
Makes 600 mL

STRAWBERRIES AND CREAM LOLLIES

300 g strawberries, washed
   and hulled
100 g caster sugar
150 mL milk
150 mL cream

1 Place strawberries, sugar and milk in blender on
medium speed for 30 seconds.
2 Add cream and blend on low for 30 seconds.
3 Pour into lolly moulds and freeze.
Makes 650 mL

NON-DAIRY LOLLY

2 tablespoons honey
500 mL (2 cups) soya milk
2 tablespoons carob powder
   or *carob syrup*

1 Dissolve the honey in a saucepan with soya milk.
2 Whisk in carob and chill.
3 Place in lolly containers and freeze.
Makes 500 mL

KIWI LOLLY

750 g kiwi fruit
100 g caster sugar
3–5 drops blue food
   colouring

1 Peel kiwi fruit and place in blender with sugar and
food colouring.
2 Place in lolly containers and freeze.
Makes 800 mL

ADULT ICE CREAMS

BANANA DAIQUIRI ICE CREAM

400 g bananas
150 mL lemon juice
100 mL white rum
30 mL banana liqueur
400 mL Basic Vanilla Ice
    Cream mixture (see
    recipe)

1   Peel the bananas and blend with lemon juice on high speed.
2   Reduce to medium, add rum and liqueur and blend for 30 seconds.
3   Fold banana daiquiri mix into ice cream mixture and place in machine to freeze, following the manufacturer's instructions.
Makes 1 litre

BANANA DAIQUIRI SHERBET

500 g bananas
2 tablespoons lemon juice
180 mL Sugar Syrup I (see
    recipe)
250 mL (1 cup) milk
120 mL white rum
30 mL banana liqueur

1   Place peeled bananas in blender with lemon juice.
2   Process on high speed, slowly adding sugar syrup. Blend until smooth.
3   Add milk and alcohol, and blend at medium speed for 30 seconds.
4   Pour into your ice cream maker and freeze, following the manufacturer's instructions.
Makes 1 litre

CALVADOS SORBET

100 mL Calvados
500 mL (2 cups) Sugar
    Syrup I (see recipe)
250 mL (1 cup) apple juice
100 mL water

This is an easy dish. Simply place all ingredients in the ice cream maker and freeze, following the manufacturer's instructions.
Makes 1 litre

TIA MARIA AND HAZELNUT ICE CREAM

6 egg yolks (50 g)
150 g granulated sugar
500 mL (1 cup) milk
200 mL cream
100 mL Tia Maria
100 g hazelnuts, toasted and
    chopped

1   In a double saucepan, whisk eggs and sugar over boiling water until thick and white.
2   Heat milk until it simmers. Pour into egg mix and stir over hot water until thickened.
3   Cool, add cream and Tia Maria.
4   Place the mixture in your ice cream maker and freeze, following the manufacturer's instructions, for about 15 minutes.
5   When the mixture is half frozen, add the hazelnuts and continue freezing until solid.
Makes 1 litre

Left to right: Canadian Freeze; Banana and Yoghurt Popsicles;
Strawberries and Cream Lollies; Kiwi Lolly and Non-dairy Lolly

CREME DE MENTHE ICE CREAM

60 mL creme de menthe
1 egg (65 g)
80 g caster sugar
1 teaspoon vanilla essence
725 mL cream
125 mL (½ cup) milk

1   Place all ingredients *except* 700 mL cream in a blender and process for 30 seconds on low speed.
2   Process again, slowly adding the 700 mL cream.
3   Place in your ice cream maker and freeze, following the manufacturer's instructions.
Note: The alcohol will slow down freezing.
Makes approximately 1 litre

PERNOD ICE CREAM

60 mL Pernod
1 egg (65 g)
665 mL cream
125 mL (½ cup) milk
150 g caster sugar
1 tablespoon vanilla essence

1   Place the Pernod, egg, 125 mL (½ cup) cream, milk, sugar and vanilla in a blender and process on medium speed for 30 seconds.
2   Add 600 mL cream and blend for a further 30 seconds.
3   Place in your ice cream maker and freeze, following the manufacturer's instructions.
Note: Any anise liqueur such as anisette or sambuca, can be used in place of Pernod.
Makes approximately 1 litre

RUM RAISIN ICE CREAM

100 g raisins
180 mL dark rum
100 mL boiling water
1 egg (65 g)
600 mL cream
125 mL (½ cup) milk
150 g sugar
1 tablespoon vanilla essence

From top clockwise: Three adult ices — Rum Raisin Ice Cream;
Creme de Menthe Ice Cream and Pernod Ice Cream

1   Combine raisins, rum and boiling water in a bowl, stir and leave overnight to infuse.

2   Pour the liquid from the raisins into a blender with the egg, 125 mL cream, milk, sugar and vanilla, and blend on low speed for 30 seconds.

3   Continue to blend a further 30 seconds while adding the remaining cream.

4   Place mixture in your ice cream maker and add the raisins only when the mixture is half frozen.

Makes approximately 1.5 litres

CHAMPAGNE SORBET

300 mL Sugar Syrup I (see
   recipe)
550 mL brut champagne or
   extra dry sparkling wine
1 teaspoon lemon juice
2 egg whites

1   Combine sugar syrup, champagne and lemon juice, and place in your ice cream maker for 15 minutes.
2   Beat egg whites and fold into mixture.
3   Continue churning until frozen.
Makes 900 mL

KENTUCKY DERBY SORBET

50 g mint leaves
250 g (1 cup) sugar
500 mL (2 cups) water
150 mL bourbon
30 mL creme de menthe

1   Place mint leaves and half the sugar in a blender and blend until well combined.
2   Remove and place in pan with remaining sugar and water.
3   Bring to the boil, stirring occasionally, and simmer for 10 minutes. Strain and chill.
4   Add creme de menthe and bourbon. Put mixture in your ice cream maker and freeze, following the manufacturer's instructions.
Makes 1 litre

PORRIDGE AND WHISKY ICE CREAM

200 g rolled oats
600 mL cream
250 g moist brown sugar
100 mL whisky

1   Toast the oats under the grill until lightly brown; cool.
2   Place the cream and sugar in a blender for 30 seconds at medium speed. Add the whisky.
3   Pour over the oats and combine.
4   Place the mixture in your ice cream maker and freeze, following the manufacturer's instructions.
Makes 1 litre

MANDARIN SHERBET

12 mandarins
300 mL Sugar Syrup I (see
   recipe)
2 tablespoons lemon juice
100 mL orange juice
   concentrate
90 mL Bols mandarin
   liqueur
2 egg whites

1   Wash the mandarins and grate the peel finely.
2   Add the fine zest to the sugar syrup, bring to the boil and refrigerate overnight.
3   Juice the mandarins, strain and add to the sugar syrup.
4   Add the lemon juice, orange juice concentrate and liqueur and place the mixture in your ice cream maker for 15 minutes.
5   Beat egg whites to a soft peak, add to the mixture and freeze another 15–20 minutes.
Makes 500 mL

MAINSTAY PINA COLADA

300 g fresh pineapple
250 g caster sugar
175 g coconut cream
1 egg (65 g)
450 mL cream
150 mL Mainstay (white
   cane spirit)

1   Peel, core and chop the pineapple.
2   Blend at high speed with the sugar and coconut cream.
3   Slow blender to medium, add egg, cream and Mainstay, and blend a further 30 seconds.
4   Place in your ice cream maker and freeze, following the manufacturer's instructions.
Makes 1 litre

Kentucky Derby Sorbet and Mandarin Sherbet

PEACH AND CHAMPAGNE SORBET

150 g caster sugar
500 g peaches
juice ½ lemon
150 mL champagne
sponge fingers, for serving

1   Place sugar in saucepan with ¼ cup water. Simmer, stirring to dissolve sugar. Set aside to cool.

2   Place peaches in sufficient boiling water to cover and simmer 1½ minutes.

3   Peel, remove stones and cut flesh into chunks. Sprinkle with lemon juice and then puree.

4   Whisk peach puree and cooled syrup together.

5   Pour mixture into your ice cream maker and freeze, following the manufacturer's instructions.

6   Chill serving glasses. Immediately before serving place 2 scoops of peach sorbet in each glass and pour champagne over. Serve with sponge fingers.

Makes 500 mL

NECTARINE ICE CREAM WITH FRESH NECTARINES

3 large nectarines
375 mL (1½ cups) cream
*1 tablespoon Grand
   Marnier*
125 g (½ cup) sugar

*65 mL (¼ cup) Sugar Syrup
   I (see recipe)*
*1 tablespoon chopped
   pistachio nuts, to garnish*

1   Pour boiling water over 1 nectarine in a bowl. Stand 1 minute, drain, plunge into cold water then remove skin and stone the fruit. Puree to make ½ cup.

2   Combine puree with cream, 2 teaspoons Grand Marnier and sugar in a food processor and blend until smooth and the sugar is dissolved. Pour into your ice cream maker and freeze, following the manufacturer's instructions.

3   Just before serving, peel the remaining nectarines (as described previously) and cut each into 8 slices. Place in a bowl and baste with 2 tablespoons of sugar syrup and the remaining Grand Marnier. Cover to prevent fruit discolouring.

4   Place 2 scoops ice cream in individual bowls and arrange the fruit slices in a fan shape. Top with pistachio nuts and serve with sponge finger biscuits.

Serves 6

BROWN BREAD ICE CREAM

*250 g fresh brown
   breadcrumbs*
200 g brown sugar
650 mL cream
90 mL dark rum

1   Remove crusts from wholemeal loaf, cut crumb in pieces and feed into blender.

2   Place in shallow baking tray and mix in sugar thoroughly.

3   Put in preheated oven at 200°C (400°F) and stir every 5 minutes for 30 minutes; cool.

4   Break up the sugar-bread mix into crumbs again.

5   Add cream and rum and place in your ice cream maker. Freeze, following the manufacturer's instructions.

Makes 1 litre

Nectarine Ice Cream with fresh nectarines

Peach and Champagne Sorbet

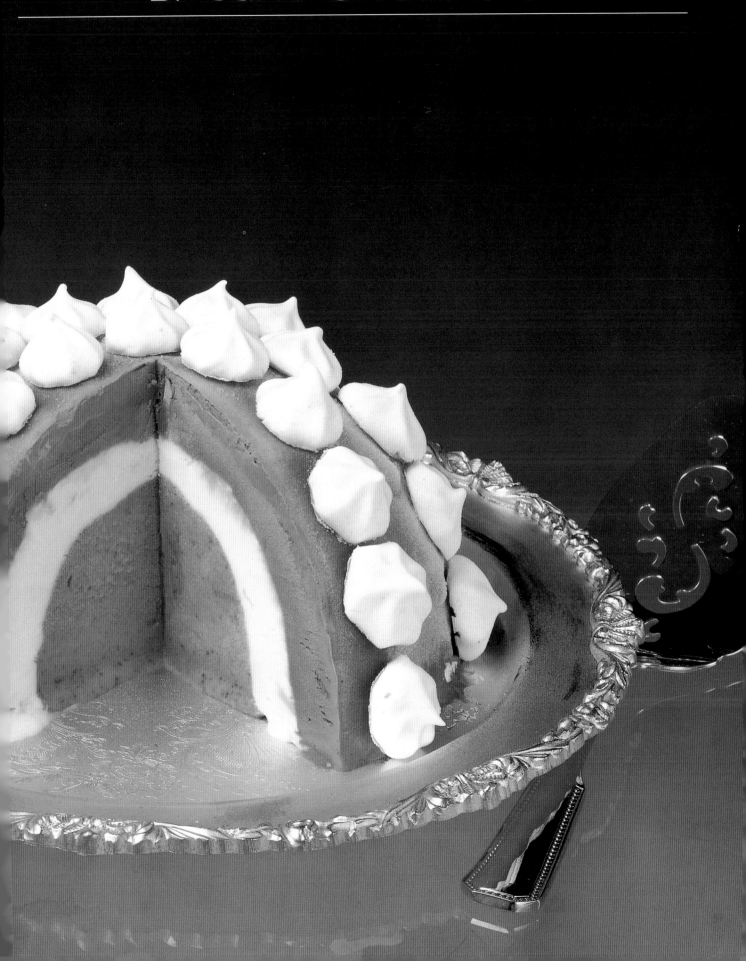

Now you have realised how simple it is to make ice cream, you may want to creat new gastronomic delights for celebrating special occasions.

We have included several desserts that are remarkably simple yet will delight your family and friends. Perhaps the most delicious is Bombe Alaska which, if you ordered it in a restaurant, would be brought flaming to your table and presented as the ultimate in desserts. Named also Baked Alaska or Norwegian Omelette, this dish is made easily from sponge cake, fruit, ice cream and meringue.

EASY ICE CREAM BOMBE ALASKA

1 litre chocolate ice cream
1 litre vanilla ice cream
1 litre strawberry ice cream

MERINGUE
4 egg whites (65 g)
¼ teaspoon cream of tartar
100 g granulated sugar

1   Soften chocolate ice cream in refrigerator for 30 minutes, then spread a 3 cm thick layer inside container and freeze.

2   Soften vanilla ice cream, spread a layer inside chocolate layer and freeze.

3   Soften strawberry ice cream, fill remainder of container and freeze for 4 hours or overnight.

4   To make the meringue: Beat egg whites and cream of tartar in a large mixing bowl to form soft peaks. Gradually add the sugar and beat to form stiff peaks. (The meringue can be placed in the refrigerator for 30–45 minutes.)

5   Remove ice cream from freezer. Unmould and smooth chocolate surface.

6   Spread meringue over top and sides with a spatula. Alternatively, pipe meringue rosettes over it.

7   Place in freezer for at least 1 hour. The bombe can be covered with plastic wrap and stored in freezer for up to 3 days.

8   To serve, preheat oven to 275°C (530°F). Bake until meringue is golden, 3–5 minutes. Serve immediately. *Optional flame:* The dessert can be flamed with brandy. Heat brandy, ignite and pour over.

Serves 6–8

1   *Insert a layer of chocolate ice cream into a bowl and freeze; then add vanilla ice cream layer and freeze; finally fill centre with strawberry and freeze*

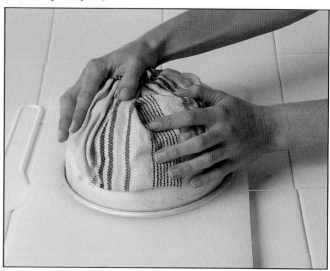

2   *Using a hot towel, carefully unmould onto a serving plate.*

3   *Smooth the chocolate surface with a spatula*

BOMBE ALASKA

1 Genoese sponge cake,
    bought or home made (see
    recipe)
125 mL (½ cup) Sugar
    Syrup I (see recipe)
100 mL liqueur (kirsch,
    cherry brandy or curaçao)
    or strawberry or
    raspberry jam
100 g chopped mixed glace
    fruits
1 litre ice cream, preferably
    vanilla

MERINGUE
4 egg whites (65 g)
¼ teaspoon cream of tartar
100 g granulated sugar

1 Cut corners off sponge and trim to oval shape. With a serrated knife, cut in half and put one half on serving platter and the other on foil.
2 Combine sugar syrup and liqueur and use 150 mL to brush both halves of cake. Place them in freezer for 1 hour. Pour remaining syrup in a bowl with fruit.
3 Remove ice cream from freezer to soften in refrigerator for 30 minutes. When ready, drain fruit and mix gently into ice cream.
4 Take cake from freezer, spread the ice cream mixture on serving platter half and place the other half on top to form a sandwich.
5 Freeze for 4 hours or overnight.
6 To make the meringue, in a large mixing bowl beat the egg whites and cream of tartar to form soft peaks. Gradually add the sugar and beat to form stiff peaks. (The meringue can be placed in the refrigerator for 30–45 minutes.)
7 Remove the sponge from the freezer and with a spatula spread the meringue over the top and sides. Alternatively you can decoratively pipe the meringue on.
8 Place in freezer for at least 1 hour. The Bombe can be covered with plastic cling wrap and stay in freezer for up to 3 days.
9 To serve, preheat oven to 275°C (530°F). Bake until meringue is golden, 3–5 minutes. Serve immediately.
Optional flame: the dessert can be flamed with brandy heated to just below boiling point, ignited and poured over.
Serves 6–8

GENOESE SPONGE CAKE

4 eggs (65 g)
100 g caster sugar
100 g flour
50 g clarified butter, very
    soft, almost melted

1 Line 2 x 22 cm sandwich tins with greaseproof paper.
2 Place the eggs and sugar in a bowl and whisk until thick and light.
3 Carefully fold in the sifted flour.
4 Pour in the butter, gently incorporating it into the mixture.
5 Bake in preheated oven at 200°C (400°F) for 30–35 minutes.
6 Cool slightly. Turn out from tin and place on wire rack, removing paper.
Serves 6–8

FRIED CREPES

CREPES
80 g flour
pinch salt
30 g butter, melted
2 eggs (65 g) beaten
150 mL milk

FILLING
1–1½ litres ice cream
2 tablespoons pureed or
    chopped fresh fruit

COATING
1 egg (65 g)
1½ tablespoons milk
1 cup finely crushed nuts,
    biscuits or cereal

1 Sift the flour and salt into a bowl.
2 Form a well and pour in butter and eggs. Stir until smooth. Add milk slowly to make a smooth batter.
3 Stand for 2 hours.
4 Heat crepe pan with small amount of butter or oil.
5 Spoon in 3 tablespoons batter. Tilt pan so batter coats surface. Cook on medium heat 1 minute. Turn over and cook on other side 1 minute.
6 Place ice cream and fruit on one half of crepe and fold over other half to seal.
7 Dip in combined egg and milk, then dip into crushed nuts; repeat process once.
8 Freeze for 1 hour then deep-fry each crepe for 10 seconds and serve immediately.
Makes 10–12

GELATO PRONTO

This is an Italian favourite with layers of ice cream, chocolate sauce and cream.

30 g dark or cooking
  chocolate
30 g milk chocolate or coffee
  flavoured chocolate
2 tablespoons custard
  powder
125 g caster sugar
120 g cocoa powder
600 mL milk
1 teaspoon vanilla essence
375 mL (1½ cups) thickened
  cream
125 g whole blanched
  almonds

TOPPING
150 mL cream
1 tablespoon caster sugar
few drops vanilla essence
60 g dark or cooking
  chocolate

1   Grate 30 g dark chocolate into 1 mixing bowl, and milk chocolate into another.
2   Dissolve custard powder, sugar and cocoa in 150 mL milk. Heat rest of milk in a pan. Stir in custard mixture and cook for 3 minutes, beating constantly. Add vanilla.
3   Remove from heat and divide custard between the 2 mixing bowls containing grated chocolate. Stir custard in each one until chocolate is melted.
4   Allow custard mixtures to cool, beating from time to time to prevent a skin forming.
5   In another bowl, beat cream until thick. When custards are almost cold, beat half the cream into each one.
6   Pour the contents of 1 bowl into your ice cream maker and freeze, following the manufacturer's instructions. Let the other bowl stand in the refrigerator meantime.
7   Freeze the second bowl of mixture in the machine.
8   To make topping, beat cream with sugar and vanilla. Melt chocolate in the top of a double saucepan.
9   When ready to serve, divide scoops of ice cream between 6 ice cream glasses, mixing the 2 flavours. Arrange almonds among ice cream balls, reserving 6 for garnish.
10   Top each glass with whipped cream, pour over melted chocolate and garnish with a single almond on each. Serve immediately.
Serves 6

ICE CREAM PIE

PIE CRUST
300 g sweet biscuit crumbs
250 g walnuts, finely ground
100 g brown sugar
½ teaspoon nutmeg
175 g unsalted butter,
  melted

GARNISH
1 cup strawberries and kiwi
  fruit
½ cup nut halves
½ cup chocolate pieces

FILLING
1½–2 litres ice cream
  (chocolate, vanilla,
  strawberry or banana)

1   Combine the biscuit crumbs, nuts, sugar, spice and butter together.
2   Spread evenly on a 30 cm pie dish forming a ridge around the edge.
3   Fill the pie shell with a combination of ice creams.
4   Decorate with strawberries, kiwi fruit, nut halves and choc pieces.
5   Freeze for a minimum 3 hours, or wrap in plastic cling wrap for up to 1 week.
Serves 6-8

ICE CREAM CHARLOTTE

Perhaps one of the simplest moulded desserts, this dish can use any ice cream as a filling.

Use a complementary puree (tutti frutti, apricot, almond or mango) to pour over and add whipped cream.

12 ladyfingers, split in half
1 litre ice cream
250 mL (1 cup) fruit puree
250 mL (1 cup) whipped
  cream

1   Line the bottom and sides of a 1.5 litre charlotte mould with the biscuits, placing the rounded sides toward the mould.
2   Where necessary, cut the biscuits to ensure a tight fit, trimming any that extend over the mould.
3   Remove the ice cream from the freezer to soften slightly.
4   Spoon into the mould, pressing against the ladyfingers until filled to the top — cover with plastic wrap.
5   Return to freezer for 3 hours.
6   To serve, invert mould to remove charlotte onto a serving dish.
Serves 6-8

Ice Cream Pie

PARTY CASSATA

1 litre vanilla ice cream
1 litre chocolate ice cream

FILLING
125 mL (½ cup) cream
1 tablespoon angelica,
   chopped
1 tablespoon sultanas
1 tablespoon mixed peel
12 almonds, slivered
12 glace cherries, sliced
2 tablespoons icing sugar

1   Lightly grease a 1.25 litre mould or pudding basin with oil. Put a disc of oiled foil or paper in the base. Place the basin in the freezer.

2   Soften vanilla ice cream and line the prepared mould with it, using a round-bowled spoon for spreading. Freeze until firm — about 1 hour.

3   Again work with a spoon to soften the chocolate ice cream, making it pliable. Make a second lining of ice cream in the mould or basin. Cover and freeze until firm.

4   To make the filling, whip the cream and fold in the prepared fruit and sifted icing sugar.

5   Fill the ice cream-lined mould with the cream-fruit mixture and replace in the freezer.

6   Take out of freezer about 30 minutes before serving. Turn out with care, and leave in refrigerator for the remaining time before serving.

Note: We have made this recipe with vanilla and chocolate ice cream. It will be equally delicious however, made using coffee, strawberry or your favourite flavours.

Serves 8–10

ICE CREAM SANDWICH

In this recipe we bake a biscuit, spread ice cream on it, place another biscuit over it and dip in chocolate.

1½ litres vanilla ice cream

BISCUIT
225 g softened butter
225 g brown sugar
2 eggs (65 g)
1 teaspoon vanilla essence
275 g flour
35 g cocoa powder
1 teaspoon baking powder
½ teaspoon nutmeg
¼ teaspoon salt

CHOCOLATE
120 g cooking chocolate
125 mL (½ cup) condensed
   milk

1   Preheat oven to 200°C (400°F).

2   Cream butter and sugar in bowl until light and fluffy, then mix in remaining ingredients to make a dough.

3   On floured surface roll dough to 5 mm thick and cut into 7.5 cm shapes.

4   Place on greased tray and bake 10–15 minutes; when cooked, cool on rack.

5   Heat cooking chocolate and condensed milk together in double boiler to melt.

6   Soften vanilla ice cream. Spread on biscuit and place another biscuit on top.

7   Hold between 2 forks and dip in chocolate; place on greaseproof paper and serve once the chocolate has set.

Serving Suggestion: To make a cake merely cut the dough in 2 x 30 cm shapes and bake.

Serves 12

Fried Ice Cream

FRIED ICE CREAM

1 litre vanilla ice cream
1 egg (65 g)
1½ tablespoons milk
1 cup finely crushed nuts,
  biscuits or cereal
oil, for deep-frying

1   Line a tray with greaseproof paper.
2   Scoop out 8–12 individual balls of ice cream.
3   Place on tray and freeze 1 hour.
4   Beat the egg and milk together, place crumbling mix in a bowl.
5   Quickly dip the ice cream in the egg and milk mixture then the crumbling mix, repeat and freeze 1 hour.
6   Heat oil to 190°C, drop in balls individually and brown approximately 10 seconds. Remove and serve.
Makes 8–12

ICE CREAM CHOCOLATE CUPS

These chocolate cups are a good way to dress up ice cream for a special occasion. Put a single scoop of any flavour ice cream in each cup. Chocolate Mint is particularly good, especially with a splash of creme de menthe.

300 g chocolate,
  coarsely chopped
50 g butter, softened
1 litre ice cream

1   Melt chocolate over low heat and stir in butter.
2   Place 2 paper patty cases together and paint the inside with chocolate.
3   Chill for 5 minutes, then repeat twice and place in freezer.
4   When ready to serve, peel paper cup gently from chocolate.
Serves 8–10

CHOCOLATE ROLL

No, not a banana roll but a rolled out sheet of cake mixture spread with jam and ice cream.

*1–1½ litres vanilla ice
   cream.*

SPONGE
*125 g (1 cup) flour
1 teaspoon baking soda
¼ teaspoon salt
3 eggs, separated
100 g caster sugar
60 g unsalted butter, melted
65 mL (¼ cup) molasses
30 g cocoa powder
1 tablespoon nutmeg
3 tablespoons water*

1   Preheat the oven to 190°C (375°F).
2   Line a sandwich tin with greaseproof paper.
3   Sift the flour, baking soda and salt together.
4   Beat the egg yolks in a double-boiler with an electric mixer, gradually adding the sugar until thick and light coloured.
5   Remove from the heat, adding butter, molasses, cocoa, nutmeg and water.
6   Fold in flour mixture.
7   Beat egg whites until stiff, fold into the batter and pour into tin.
8   Bake for 10–12 minutes. Cool 1 minute and turn onto a tea towel.
9   Remove paper and roll as for Swiss roll; cool.
10   When cool, soften the ice cream by placing it in the refrigerator for 30 minutes.
11   Unroll the cake and quickly spread the ice cream about 2.5 cm thick.
12   Reroll the cake, place on a non-stick pan and freeze for 2 hours minimum.

Serving Suggestion: Place a 2.5 cm slice of roll on fruit puree such as strawberry, and sprinkle with icing sugar.

Serves 8–10

PROFITEROLES

These light pastries are made with choux pastry, the same pastry used to make eclairs. When cooled, pipe softened ice cream into them instead of custard, dip in chocolate and serve.

2 litres ice cream

PUFF BALLS
*240 mL water
115 g butter, cut in pieces
150 g flour
¼ teaspoon salt
4 eggs*

CHOCOLATE
*120 g cooking chocolate
125 mL (½ cup) condensed
   milk*

1   Preheat oven to 220°C (425°F) and place greaseproof paper on an oven tray.
2   Heat water and butter in saucepan, stir and bring to the boil.
3   Reduce heat to low. Add flour and salt, stirring until the dough forms a ball and leaves the side of the pan.
4   Remove from the heat and beat in the eggs one at a time, beating well between each addition.
5   Place dough in piping bag, and pipe mounds about 4 cm in diameter onto tray.
6   Bake for 15 minutes, turn down to 200°C (400°F) and leave in the oven for 15 minutes with the door ajar.
7   Make a slit in the side of the puff balls and pipe in softened ice cream.
8   Melt cooking chocolate and condensed milk together in the top of a double boiler.
9   Dip balls in melted chocolate and serve immediately.

Makes 20–24

*From top to bottom: Ice Cream Chocolate Cups; Profiteroles and
Chocolate Roll*

Fresh Fruit (Strawberry) and Chocolate Sauces

SAUCES AND TOPPINGS

While delicious on its own, your homemade ice creams can be enhanced or complemented by many extras. Toppings and sauces can be made ahead of time and chilled or heated to suit.

The simplest and probably also most colourful are the fruit sauces, purees or coulis. One basic recipe can serve as the foundation for all of these.

FRESH FRUIT SAUCE

1 kg prepared fresh fruit or
canned fruit drained of
syrup. Use strawberries,
raspberries, kiwi fruit
and pineapple
600 g sugar

Place fruit and sugar in blender or food processor and blend on medium/low speed for approximately 2–5 minutes to puree and dissolve sugar.

Makes 1.5 litres

CHOCOLATE SAUCE

20 g caster sugar
350 mL milk
120 mL cream
40 g unsalted butter, melted
200 g cooking chocolate

1 Place the sugar, milk, cream and melted butter in a saucepan and stir to dissolve.
2 Bring to the boil then add to the chocolate.
3 Pour back into the saucepan, boil then cool.
4 Serve cold.
Makes 750 mL

COOROONA CARAMEL SAUCE

220 g sugar
125 mL (½ cup) glucose or
*   corn syrup*
pinch salt
125 mL (½ cup) cream

1 Place the sugar in a heavy saucepan over low heat and stir continuously until it becomes liquid and golden brown.
2 Slowly pour in the glucose, stirring rapidly.
3 Add the salt and cream and serve warm.
Makes 350 mL

BUTTERSCOTCH SAUCE

250 g brown sugar
125 mL (½ cup) glucose or
   corn syrup
60 g unsalted butter
pinch salt
60 mL water
2 teaspoons vanilla essence
100 mL cream

1 Mix the sugar, glucose, butter, salt and water in a saucepan and bring to the boil.
2 Remove from the heat and stir in the vanilla and cream.
Note: This sauce may be served warm or cold.
Makes 350 mL

COLD COFFEE SAUCE

200 g sugar
250 mL (1 cup) water
2 tablespoons coffee powder
30 g unsalted butter
125 mL (½ cup) cream

1 Combine the sugar and water in a saucepan over medium heat.
2 Stir constantly, cooking for 5 minutes.
3 Add coffee, stir to dissolve, then remove from heat.
4 Gradually stir in the butter then the cream.
5 Store in refrigerator until required.
Makes 400 mL

GINGER SAUCE

100 g sugar
100 mL vinegar
40 g chopped ginger root
375 mL (1½ cups) green
   ginger wine
squeeze lemon juice, to taste

1 In a pan combine sugar and vinegar and heat until sugar changes colour.
2 Add ginger root, ginger wine and lemon juice and stir to combine. Can be served hot or cold.
Makes 500 mL

LOU AND ANDY'S FUDGE SAUCE

125 mL cream
45 g unsalted butter
75 g granulated sugar
75 g brown sugar
pinch salt
60 g cocoa powder

1 Heat the cream and butter in a saucepan over medium heat until boiling.
2 Add white and brown sugar, gently heating to dissolve.
3 Whisk in salt and cocoa to dissolve.
4 Serve warm.
Makes 350 mL

Kiwi fruit and Cooroona Caramel Sauces

CONES

Making your own cones is as easy as making biscuits. All you need is an oven, electric mixer and a cone horn. If you don't have a cream horn tin then you can fashion a cone shape from heavy brown paper.

3 egg whites (65 g)
150 g caster sugar
75 g flour,
70 g unsalted butter, melted

1 Preheat oven to 200°C (400°F) and prepare a baking tray with greaseproof paper or lightly buttered foil.
2 Whisk the egg whites in a bowl until stiff.
3 Fold in 75 g sugar and whisk to dissolve.
4 Fold in sifted flour, butter and remaining 75 g sugar.
5 Drop spoonfuls of the mix onto tray and bake 3–5 minutes until light brown around edges.
6 Remove from tray with a flat-bladed knife and mould around greased cream horn moulds. Cool and remove.
Makes about 20

TUILLES

75 g flour
105 g sugar
2½ tablespoons ground
  almonds
vanilla essence, to taste
1½ egg whites (65 g)

OPTIONAL GARNISH
melted chocolate
ground almonds

1 Combine all ingredients in a bowl.
2 Spread mixture in thin rounds on a greased baking tray and bake at 200°C (400°F) for 6 minutes.
3 Remove from oven and form into tuille shape by allowing biscuits to droop over the handle of a wooden spoon.
4 Remove and serve, dipped if desired, in melted chocolate and ground almonds.
Makes 36

DECORATIONS

SPUN SUGAR

220 g (1 cup) caster sugar
pinch cream of tartar
125 mL (½ cup) water

1 Combine all ingredients in a small saucepan and heat, gently stirring until sugar dissolves. Using a wet pastry brush, brush away any remaining crystals from the side of pan as these will cause syrup to crystallise.
2 Increase heat and boil until a rich golden colour. Allow to cool slightly.
3 Working over sheets of baking paper dip 2 forks into syrup, join together then draw apart to form fine threads of toffee. Work quickly before toffee sets and remember that it is very hot. When all the toffee has been used, carefully lift threads from paper and place a little on top of each individual ice cream dish.
Note: Do not attempt this if the weather is humid as the spun sugar will dissolve within moments of making. Prepare just before serving.

Assorted cones and tuilles to serve with ice creams

CHOCOLATE PEPPERMINT LEAVES

Chocolate leaves are the perfect finishing touch for cakes or desserts. They also make an elegant decoration for a plate of chocolates for your dinner party. Choose leaves that are perfect, shiny and heavily veined such as gum, rose, camellia or gardenia leaves, or ivy.

leaves of your choice
150 g dark compound
 chocolate
2–3 drops peppermint oil
 flavouring

1   Clean and dry leaves.

2   Melt chocolate in the top of a double boiler and add 2–3 drops peppermint oil flavouring.

3   Paint the back of each leaf with chocolate, place on tray and freeze until set.

4   Gently peel off leaves from chocolate.

VARIATION

Use white chocolate coloured with oil-based food colouring and flavoured with other essences — for instance pale pink leaves with strawberry oil flavouring.

Chocolate Peppermint Leaves

1   Melt chocolate in a small container over hot water

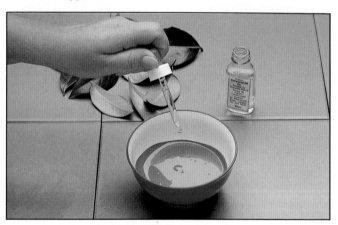

2   Add peppermint flavouring

3   Paint the back of each leaf with chocolate

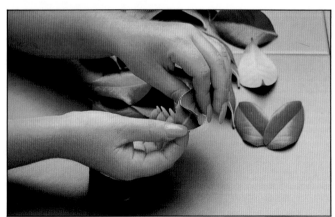

4   When set, gently peel off leaf

ALMOND PRALINE

350 g blanched almonds,
  slivered or chopped
150 mL water
500 g (2 cups) granulated
  sugar

1   Place almonds on tray in preheated 180°C (350°F) oven. Switch oven off and leave almonds there for 15–20 minutes.

2   In a heavy saucepan, over medium heat, dissolve water and sugar, stirring constantly and occasionally brushing down sides of saucepan with a wet pastry brush to remove sugar crystals. When sugar is dissolved, bring to boil for 15–18 minutes over high heat until mixture is a light caramel shade.

3   Remove saucepan from heat, dip base into cold water immediately, and quickly add warm almonds. Stir gently and pour straight onto greased oven tray.

4   Allow to cool, break into bite-sized pieces and store in an airtight container.

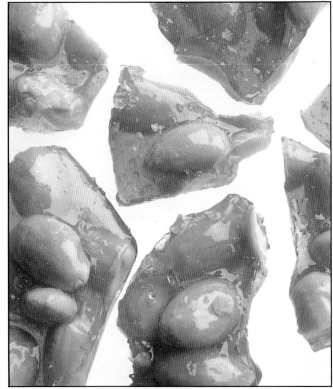

Almond Praline

1   *Put almonds in oven to warm through*

2   *Dissolve sugar in water, stirring and brushing down sides of pan*

3   *Spread over a marble slab*

4   *When cool, break into bite-sized pieces*

◊ DRINKS ◊

Iced drinks, whips, smoothies, shakes, sodas, spiders, cocktails — the list can be expanded to include any creation you can invent using a few basic ingredients. The following selection can form the basis for a lifetime of enjoying exciting and (mostly) healthy beverages.

MILKSHAKES

Milkshakes can be flavoured with fruit juice cordials or commercial syrups. The secret to making a good shake is extra cold milk (almost frozen). You need only one piece of equipment, a blender or a vitamiser.

BANANA SMOOTHIE

600 mL chilled milk
1 large banana
1 large scoop vanilla ice
   cream
10 mL honey
1 heaped teaspoon malt
   powder

1   Place all ingredients in a blender and process at high speed until the banana is puréed and the honey dissolved.
Serves 1

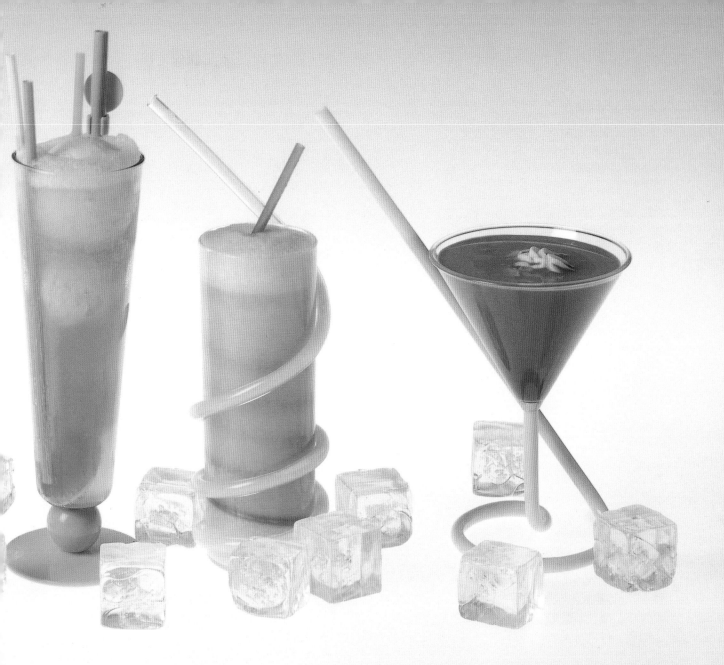

Left to right: Banana Smoothie; Chocolate Soda; Strawberry Spider; Lime Float; Skinny Shake and Iced Coffee

SOYA HEALTH DRINK

400 mL soya milk — plain
1 tablespoon carob powder
  or paste
1 tablespoon honey

1   Place all ingredients in a blender and process at high speed for 10–15 seconds. Soya milk does not beat up in volume.
Serves 1

ICED COFFEE 1

When next you make a pot of coffee and have some leftover, put it in the fridge to use for iced coffee.

750 mL percolated or filter
  coffee, chilled
250 mL (1 cup) milk
sugar, to taste

1   Combine all ingredients in a blender.
2   Serve in glasses and add 1 scoop of vanilla ice cream or pipe whipped cream and top with cinnamon.
Serves 4–6

ICED COFFEE II

For a quick iced coffee.

400 mL chilled milk
1 scoop vanilla ice cream
1 heaped teaspoon instant
    coffee

1   Combine all ingredients in a blender and process at
high speed; add sugar to taste.
Serves 1

SKINNY SHAKE

For the diet conscious, skinny shakes can be made with
skim milk and any low-joule flavouring.

350 mL skim milk
45 mL low-joule cordial

1   Blend rapidly on high speed for 10 seconds.
Serves 1

MALTED MILK

400 mL milk
1 large scoop vanilla ice
    cream
30–60 mL flavoured syrup,
    to taste
1 teaspoon malted milk

1   Place all ingredients in a blender and process at high
speed until almost doubled in volume.
Serves 1

HEALTHY DRINKS

TANGY STRAWBERRY SLUSH ICE

250 mL (1 cup) water
190 mL (¾ cup) lemon juice
220 g caster sugar
500 mL (2 cups) cleaned and
    hulled strawberries

1   Blend all ingredients until smooth.
2   Add 2 cups crushed ice to blender and pour into
jug.
Makes 1.5 litres

PRITIKIN STYLE FRUIT SHAKE

2 large bananas
500 mL (2 cups) skim milk
30 mL concentrated apple
    juice

1   Place bananas in freezer for 2 hours.
2   Remove bananas and discard skin. Place fruit in
blender with milk and juice and blend until smooth.
3   Pour into glasses.
Serves 2

BREAKFAST IN A GLASS

200 g strawberries
1 egg
250 mL (1 cup) orange juice
250 mL (1 cup) skim milk

1   Place strawberries in freezer for 3 hours.
2   Remove and place in blender with other ingredients
and process until smooth.
Makes 750 mL

PRITIKIN STYLE PINE SMASH

1 pineapple, skinned, cored
    and chopped
600 mL apple juice
2 cups crushed ice

1   Combine ingredients in a blender and process for 30
seconds.
Serves 4

YOGHURT BREAKFAST

150 mL yoghurt
juice 2 oranges
1 egg
1 tablespoon honey
1 tablespoon wheatgerm

1   Combine all ingredients in blender in the order
listed and process for 30 seconds.   *Serves 1*

SPIDERS, SODAS AND FLOATS

These old fashioned drinks have enduring appeal. All have three ingredients in common — ice cream, syrup and soda water.

SPIDER

1 scoop vanilla ice cream
45 mL flavoured syrup or
   cordial
lemonade or soda, to fill

1   Place ice cream in a glass and pour syrup over.
2   Mash the ice cream partially, pour a little lemonade over and continue mashing.
3   Rapidly pour remaining soft drink into the glass stirring continually to froth up. Serve with a straw.
Serves 1

FLOATS

45 mL flavoured syrup or
   cordial
lemonade or soda, to fill
1 scoop vanilla ice cream

1   Place the syrup in the glass, add the lemonade and float the ice cream on top. Serve with a spoon and straw.
Serves 1

CHOCOLATE SODA

60 mL chocolate syrup
30 mL chilled milk
30 mL cream
1 scoop chocolate or vanilla
   ice cream
soda water, to fill
whipped cream, to serve

1   Place the syrup, milk and cream in a glass and stir.
2   Add the soda then ice cream and top with whipped cream.
Serves 1

COCKTAILS

Ice cream, milk and cream have their place in cocktails, particularly in blended drinks. Try the following concoctions!

BREAKFAST EGG NOGG

1 egg   150 mL milk
30 mL brandy   1 scoop vanilla ice cream
30 mL Cointreau   nutmeg, to serve

1   Place ingredients in blender at high speed for 10 seconds.
2   Pour into a highball glass and sprinkle with nutmeg.
Serves 1

PINA COLADA

35 mL crushed pineapple   45 mL coconut cream
60 mL pineapple juice   1 scoop vanilla ice cream
60 mL white rum

1   Place ingredients in blender and process for 20 seconds.
2   Pour into highball glasses and if desired, add ice.
Serves 1

BRANDY ALEXANDER

125 mL coffee ice cream
15 mL brandy
15 mL creme de cacao

1   Remove the ice cream from the refrigerator for 30 minutes to soften.
2   Place in a blender with the brandy and creme de cacao and process on low-medium speed until smooth.
3   Pour into cocktail glasses and serve.
Serves 1

GOLDEN DREAM

30 mL Galliano   30 mL orange juice
30 mL Triple Sec (orange- 1 scoop vanilla ice cream
   flavoured liqueur)

1   Pour ingredients into blender and process at high speed 10–15 seconds. Pour into a champagne glass and serve.
Serves 1

Glossary of Terms

AUSTRALIA	UK	USA
Equipment and terms		
can	tin	can
frying pan	frying pan	skillet
grill	grill	broil
greaseproof paper	greaseproof paper	waxproof paper
lamington tin	oven tray, 4 cm deep	oven tray, 1 ½ in deep
paper cases	paper baking cases	
paper towel	kitchen paper	white paper towel
patty tin	patty tin	muffin pan
plastic wrap	cling film	plastic wrap
popsicle	iced lolly	popsicle
punnet	punnet	basket for 250 g fruit
sandwich tin	sandwich tin	layer cake pan
seeded	stoned	pitted
Swiss roll tin	Swiss roll tin	jelly roll pan
Ingredients		
bicarbonate of soda	bicarbonate of soda	baking soda
caster sugar	caster sugar	granulated table sugar
cornflour	cornflour	cornstarch
cream	single cream	light or coffee cream
crystallised fruit	crystallised fruit	candied fruit
desiccated coconut	desiccated coconut	shredded coconut
essence	essence	extract
flour	plain flour	all-purpose flour
glace cherry	glace cherry	candied cherry
icing sugar	icing sugar	confectioners' sugar
pawpaw	pawpaw	papaya or papaw
rock melon	ogen melon	cantaloupe
self-raising flour	self-raising flour	all-purpose flour with baking powder, 1 cup: 2 teaspoons
sultanas	sultanas	seedless white or golden raisins
tomato paste	tomato puree	tomato paste
thickened cream	double cream	heavy or whipping cream
unsalted butter	unsalted butter	sweet butter
wholemeal flour	wholemeal flour	wholewheat flour
yoghurt	natural yoghurt	unflavoured yoghurt

Measurements

Standard Metric Measures

1 cup	=	250 mL
1 tablespoon	=	20 mL
1 teaspoon	=	5 mL

All spoon measurements are level

Cup Measures

1 x 250 mL cup =	Grams	Ounces
breadcrumbs, dry	125	4 ½
soft	60	2
butter	250	8 ¾
coconut, desiccated	95	3 ½
flour, cornflour	138	4 ¾
plain or self-raising	125	4 ½
wholemeal	135	4 ¾
fruit, mixed dried	160	5 ¾
honey	360	12 ¾
sugar, caster	225	7 ¾
crystalline	250	8 ¾
icing	175	6 ¾
moist brown	170	6
nuts	125	4

If you need to substitute

Blueberries: replace with blackberries.
Fresh fruit: replace with canned or tinned fruit.
Mulberries: replace with blackcurrants.
Pecans: replace with walnuts.
Rock melons: replace with honeydew melons.
Sour cherries: replace with morello cherries.

INDEX

ACKNOWLEDGEMENTS

The publisher would like to thank the following for assistance during the photography of this book:
Black & Decker (A/Asia) Pty Ltd, Breville, Kenwood Electrical Appliances and Philips Industries Holdings Ltd for ice cream makers (page 8)
Crown Corning Ltd for tableware (page 29)
Decor Gifts for glassware (pages 10, 11, 15)
Grace Brothers Pty Ltd for cookware and tableware (pages 9, 10, 11, 12, 15, 17, 18, 24, 27, 29, 31, 32, 47, 49, 50, 51, 53, 55, 57, 58, 59, 61, 72, 83, 86, 87, 88, 89, 90, 91)
Holmegaard for tableware (pages 19, 20, 35, 37)
Jacobus for tableware (pages 57, 77)
Mikasa Tableware for tableware (page 77)
Orrefors Australia Pty Ltd for glassware (pages 24, 26, 33, 41, 64, 65, 66, 83)
Royal Worcester for tableware (page 79)
Sasaki for tableware (pages, 6, 13, 23, 42, 44, 47)
Strachan for silverware (pages 50, 51, 55, 70, 71)
Wiltshire Consolidated Ltd for cutlery (pages, 19, 70, 71, 79)

Printed in Singapore